AROUND LONDON IN 80 BEERS

80

CHRIS POLLARD

SIOBHAN MCGINN

Cogan&Mater

Published by Cogan & Mater Limited.

© Cogan & Mater Limited 2008.
Managing Editor: Tim Webb

First Published 2008

Printed in the United Kingdom at the
University Press, Cambridge.

Book design/typography: Dale Tomlinson
Typefaces: FF Strada & Village Stag
Map: John Macklin
Photographs: All photographs by Pollard & McGinn
except for a few from Paul Winder & Bart Verhaeghe.
Thanks to the brewers, venues and their agents
for also supplying images plus a special roll on the
drums to James Clay & Co, Ian Jarrett, Stonch's Beer
Blog, Zak Avery, Jeremy & Theresa, Tom & Paulette,
Chris Gill, Pierhead Wines, & James Hope-Faulkner for
practical and moral support. We miss you John White.

ISBN 978-0-9547789-2-7

KEY TO SYMBOLS

⊖ Nearest underground station
⇌ Nearest railway station
🕐 Opening hours
▥ Draught beer
🍾 Bottled beer
✠ The flag of the nation state or
▮▮ mindset from which the beer originated

Introduction

Some jobs are more difficult than others.

After the runaway success of *'Around Bruges in 80 Beers'* we decided to turn our attentions to somewhere closer to home.

In this book we have chosen 80 places in London which we think are fun and have matched each with an interesting beer that is sold there. Each place will sell many other beers and most of the beers will be sold elsewhere in London but like experimenting chefs, we suggest these pairings to take or leave.

If you are normally a lager drinker, go to the far end of the scale and try one of the massive strong, black stouts we recommend. We dare you. If you are a wine drinker, try the gueuze – you might be astonished.

London is the city of a thousand quotes and as many superlatives. Surely nowhere in the world has so many landmark buildings, hosts so many events, boasts so many great places or famous people, real and imaginary.

From Mayfair to Whitechapel, from Sherlock Holmes to Jack the Ripper from Westminster Abbey to Notting Hill Carnival, London is instantly recognisable from countless angles to a billion people, many of whom have never even been here.

This is not a guide to London, though how can you know a place without knowing where to have a beer? It is not a regular beer guide either, though it will take you to places that serve some remarkable brews. It is certainly not a guide to historic pubs – there are enough of those already and that would have been too limiting.

'Around London in 80 Beers' takes the idea of a beer guide and brings it into modern times. We wrote it for one the world's great cities and the people who visit it, whether for the weekend, for their next job or for a lifetime.

If you know London well, we hope we will tell you of places you wish you had found sooner. For visitors, we want to provide the most memorable parts of your trip. Whether you are a long-established beer nut or just a beginner, lend us your faith and let us broaden your horizons.

We hope that you enjoy using this book as much as we enjoyed researching it.

Cheers!

PODGE & SIOBHAN

Word on the street

"When a man is tired of London,
he is tired of life;
for there is in London
all that life can afford."
Samuel Johnson (1709–1784)

Dr Johnson having passed on, we asked modern day scribbler and publican Jeff Bell, creator of Stonch's Beer Blog (stonch.blogspot.com) to muse on what modern day London can afford the untired beer drinker.

There can be few places in the world with a history of brewing to rival London's. Old brewery buildings are now converted to other uses and related place names are just reminders of what's gone before. But though that's mainly in the past, there's no need to drown our sorrows. Beer is about enjoyment here and now.

This is a city that people from all around the world call home, where there's entertainment and nightlife to cater for every taste. But however cosmopolitan London becomes, beer still holds its place in the heart of our urban culture.

Nowadays there's even more going on for the malt and hop devotee in Europe's biggest metropolis. For those with an open mind and the requisite taste buds, there's never been a better time to enjoy beer in London.

The best places to get stuck in to the finest beers are no longer likely to be run by old-fashioned, stereotypical landlords. Don't expect to hear quotes from the *Daily Mail,* or see bickering EastEnders types serving each other divorce papers on Christmas Day. Your hosts are likely to have travelled to the far-flung places from where your speciality beer was shipped.

Their enthusiasm for beer is all-important but yours is essential too. They should take the subject as seriously you do, devoting care and attention to offering a balanced repertoire to suit and expand every palate. Printed beer menus, with descriptions to match the weightiest of wine lists, are no longer uncommon, though an old-fashioned blackboard allows for a rotating range and better reflects the beery *zeitgeist*. Tarted-up or dressed-down, there's room for all sorts.

Beer that tastes good will sell itself, but the right setting is essential. That's why pubs from the bad old days – when bland beer held sway – no longer cut it. Sure, better examples of the trad jazz approach still work. For proof,

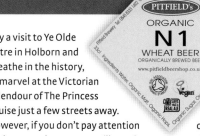

pay a visit to Ye Olde Mitre in Holborn and breathe in the history, or marvel at the Victorian splendour of The Princess Louise just a few streets away. However, if you don't pay attention to the up-and-comers, you'll restrict yourself to a dwindling band of essentially backward-looking boozers.

Looking out across the rooftops and to the future, Smith's of Smithfield is a four floor, loft-styled bar and restaurant complex by London's old meat market. Cafe Prague in Shoreditch looks nothing like a pub, but proud beer fonts and packed fridges offer the kind of Czech beer only whispered about two decades ago. The Rake Bar in Borough Market lets the beer do the talking – with minimal decor and little room for airborne felines, happy drinkers spill out onto the patio.

You don't any longer have to compromise your other passions to enjoy the very best beer. Bloomsbury Lanes is an underground centre of understated cool, where American-style bowling can be enjoyed without resorting to swill that Homer Simpson might drink. Phenomenal sea food at The Fish Shop in Clerkenwell pairs perfectly with bottle conditioned ale. After a jaunt around the Tate Modern, adjourn to its café for a London-brewed porter. At The Roxy, one of London's best independent cinemas, you can relax in front of the screen with a first-class brew in hand.

People with the savvy to seek out true cultural experiences demand the best, and that extends to the contents of their pint glass.

The ebb and flow of the brewpub tide has been a feature of the London beer scene since entrepreneur David Bruce opened his first Firkin here in 1979.

At the time of writing, we're left with only five pubs and bars where beer is brewed on-site, where a year ago there were seven: not an impressive number for a city of this size. Nonetheless, the venues in which this grassroots brewing takes place speak volumes about the changed status of beer. All offer strictly contemporary decor, from the neo-industrial Bunker Bierhall in Covent Garden to the stripped white walls of The Horseshoe in Hampstead village. Down at The Florence in Herne Hill, no expense was spared on the refit of what was a dingy Irish theme pub. In the open kitchen, busy chefs can be seen using the house brews to add an individual touch to their recipes. Brewpubs bring the wonderful aromas of brewing and the wonder of fermentation closer to the drinker, promoting understanding of and enthusiasm for our favourite beverage. As such, these *vanguardistes* are to be encouraged and supported.

No longer is beer the esoteric interest of the beardy-weirdy few. Half the fun of learning about what's on offer from books like this is passing on the good news and taking others on the journey with you. Advise your fellow travellers that they can leave the anoraks at home, and footwear need not be sensible. Enjoy.

JEFF BELL
Stonch.blogspot.com

London's world of beer

Had we tried to compile this book twenty years ago, it is unlikely we would have found eighty places in London, each selling a different, interesting beer. If we had, then most of them would have been pubs and virtually every beer a traditional draught English ale, mainly from within a hundred miles of London.

Only the crazed and the stupid foresaw a world in which craft beer brewing would return as an international phenomenon, or that beer would have become the stuff of as many personal passions and shared interests, essential knowledge and common misunderstanding as wine, cheese, bread, seasonal foods and every other consumable that comes in drab and delightful forms.

Compiling now, fewer than half the beers we feature here are traditional draught, or 'real' ales and many of those come from the furthest outposts of Britain. Over a third are imported. Yet each is a great brew in its own right. We consider no 'wet air' brands here.

English ales

The English beer revolution began in the 1970s with the emergence of a lobby of malcontents who objected to the efforts being made by large national breweries to foist heavily advertised, easy-to-make, 'keg' beers on a generation that, having known neither rationing nor war, were less compliant.

The Scots and Welsh followed in the 1980s and the Irish are still thinking about it.

Against international economic trends, small, family-owned local breweries became unwitting heroes in a battle of everyman against the forces of conformity.

The smaller brewers did not always have quality on their side but they did have individuality. The larger companies undoubtedly made beers that were reliably consistent and crystal clear but these were their only major assets. Impressive flavour or character was not – their advisors said it put people off.

For the next quarter century, good British beer was synonymous with 'real ale'. People with no yen for good beer drank locally made big name lager instead.

But beer drinkers, like every other cosmopolitan group in the developed world, started to travel. When they did, with varying degrees of reluctance, they had to admit that there were other beer styles out there that were pretty good too.

Belgian ales

Of all the places to attract the attention of knowledgeable British beer drinkers it was Belgium that became the most revered.

The small kingdom across the North Sea, once described by De Gaulle as 'invented by the British to annoy the French' makes over a thousand different brands of beer in more than twenty major categories, some uniquely Belgian, and in an estimated 400 sub-styles.

These range from table beers with virtually no alcohol to heavyweight barley wines, from jet black stouts to straw-coloured wheat beers, from spiced sweet ales to beers rendered acid by fermentation in oak tuns for several years.

60% of beer made in Belgium is now exported but although it would be possible for a London bar owner to source hundreds of different brands, the UK remains a relatively small market for Belgian producers.

Deutsche Bieren

Germany is famous for producing lagers, though distinctive German styles such as *Kölsch* from Cologne (Köln), *Altbier* from Düsseldorf and the very different types of wheat beer from Berlin and Bavaria are all in fact ales.

The critical difference in German beers is the residual influence of the now defunct *Reinheitsgebot* or 'Beer Purity Law', which dictated that only malted grain, hops, water and yeast could be used to make beer.

London's better known German lagers are unlikely to pass the purity

test nowadays and, uncharacteristically for German businesses, some of the best of the rest have a way to go before they become efficient exporters.

Pivo České

The Russian occupation of Czechoslovakia, which began in 1948, had two effects on Czech breweries. It reduced necessary investment on upkeep and modernisation of kit while on the other hand protecting them from takeover and closure.

When the Velvet revolution came in 1989, the initially explosive effect of free market economics enabled Czech brewing to find its rightful place in the world.

This was rapidly tempered by international players buying up many of the best lager producers and dumbing down their products, at the same time purloining their names to add contemporary credibility to a range of otherwise dull lagers.

Things have settled down a bit now and Czech lagers in blond and brown incarnations are making their way to London in increasing volumes.

American micros

Prize for the most improved brewing nation of the last thirty years goes without question to the US. Though to be fair it could hardly have got much worse.

Industrial producers of low-strength, tinned blond rice beers abounded in the US long before the rest of the world succumbed to them.

London's world of beer

With nowhere else to go, American home brewers started to imitate the styles of beer their forefathers had made and which they still encountered themselves on tours round Europe.

Thirty years on there are nearly 1500 new commercial breweries in the US, many producing world class craft beers that now set the standard for longer established beer cultures, reviving the great beers of the world and inventing a fair few on the way.

Eurobières

France's north eastern *départements* now muster over sixty craft breweries, many making beers that are giving the Belgians something to think about. The Bretons have invented a unique type of black, porterish wheat beer and even the Mediterranean island of Corsica is in on the act.

It is only a matter of time before the forty or so new craft brewers of Italy organise themselves a London enclave. The Eastern Europeans are already here in small numbers, with big black brews from Poland attracting attention. Roll on Estonian porter.

On the other side of the Baltic Scandinavia now has over 100 new breweries. In Norway in particular, punitive taxes on alcohol led small producers to reason that if a dreary brand name lager costs a small fortune, people will pay a little extra for something memorable. Watch out for some huge IPAs and Imperial Stouts in the not too distant future.

Wherever next?

Great craft beers are already being made by hundreds of breweries in Canada, Australia and New Zealand, Austria, Switzerland and Slovenia, Argentina, Japan and Vietnam. What began as an English obsession appears to have spread across the globe.

But in the way of these things interest has also refocused closer to home.

Shortly before London's favourite local brewer Youngs disappeared up to Bedford, their head brewer headed down to St Austell in Cornwall, where an impressive list of achievements has included commissioning a special Cornish malt and securing national distribution for the peninsula's beers.

The Scottish beer revival, obvious in almost every bar north of the border, is starting to entertain Londoners too.

All we need now is to see a return of brewers to London. Let us hope that concerns about transport costs and the environment make this possible by our next edition.

Prost!

TIM WEBB

Cogan&Mater
Publishers of the world's greatest beers

CAMRA's Great British Beer Festival

CAMPAIGN FOR REAL ALE

It may not be as awesomely huge as Munich's Oktoberfest but then it is not an industry megasplurge either.

It may not show quite as many brews as Denver's Great American but at least you get served more than a thimbleful when you ask for a beer.

It may not have the garage chic of Brussels' Bruxellensis but garages don't come much bigger than Earl's Court and it is Britain's largest beer festival by far.

What is remarkable about the Great British Beer Festival (**www.gbbf.org.uk**) it that it has been going for over thirty years, dependent entirely on the good will of legions of mildly eccentric, beer-obsessed volunteers on holiday.

In the first full week of August, from Tuesday evening to Saturday afternoon, in the Earls Court Exhibition Centre, get to try countless hundreds of 'real' ales served mainly direct from the cask. Don't miss the Bières Sans Frontières bar either, with over a hundred fine beers from round the world.

Plus a wide range of better bar food, an eclectic range of music and as broad a range of beer drinkers as you will encounter anywhere on the planet.

North and Central London

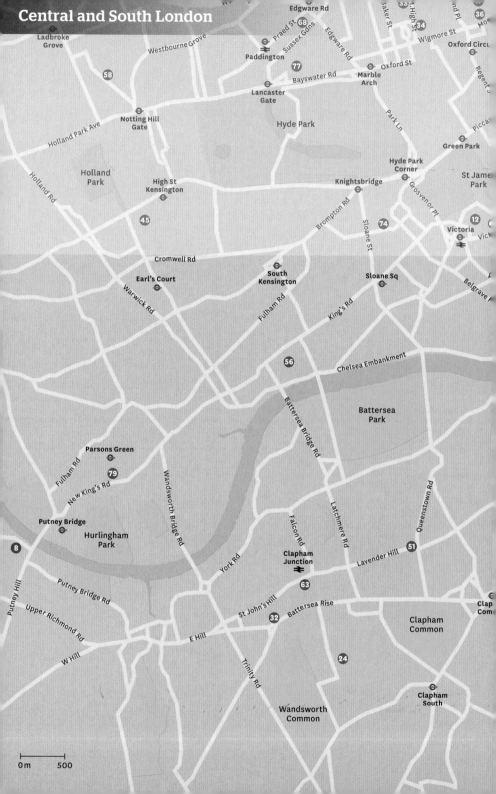

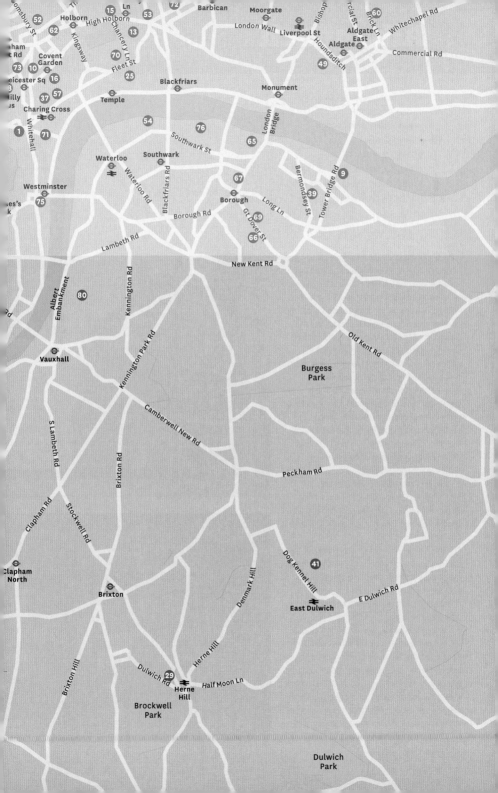

Albannach

66 Trafalgar Square WC2N 5DS
T 020 7930 0066
www.albannach.co.uk
Charing Cross
CLOSED SUNDAY
others 12.00–01.00
Innis & Gunn Cask Aged Ale (6.6%)
Innis & Gunn Brewing Co., Edinburgh, Scotland

If the Scottish parliament ever elects to open a London consulate they should seriously consider putting an office above this temple of Caledonian chic on Trafalgar Square, with its panoramic view of Nelson's column.

If your Scotland includes images of Mel Gibson in a blue face-pack, deep-fried Mars bars and raddled consumers with talons gripped to a tin of superstrength lager then come to be educated by the Albannach.

No Clydeside theme pub this. The bar, restaurant and cocktail room are spread over three storeys of contemporary design with prime Scottish ingredients. There is even a Highland hunting lodge allusion with this urban cavern illuminated by a massive antler chandelier.

Expect Arbroath smokie mousse, Perthshire-sourced rack of lamb, smoked Shetlands salmon, a board of craft Scottish cheeses and ice cream made with 12-year-old Chivas Regal.

The whisky sommelier may have felt he could spare that from his menu of 200 malts, including two from the mythical Port Ellen distillery of Islay. Customers are advised to check their mortgage facility before settling down for the night.

Draught beer is represented by Deuchars IPA but our featured ale is from a clear bottle. Brewed at the Belhaven Brewery in Dunbar, Innis & Gunn's beer is transferred to a bonded warehouse where it is aged for eleven weeks in oak Bourbon casks. The result is a unique copper-coloured beer with a heavy aroma of vanilla, its initial toffee-malt flavour giving way to a prolonged oaky sweetness.

Bar Music Hall

134 Curtain Road EC2A 3AR
T 020 7613 5951
www.barmusichall.com
Old Street
Fri & Sat 11.00–02.00
others 11.00–24.00
Duvel (8.5%)
Brouwerij Duvel Moortgat, nr Antwerp, Belgium

Provincial types beware. What was once genuinely a music hall is now a self-styled 'funky European café bar', which means better modern British with a Belgian twist. Found in deepest fashionable Shoreditch, the centrepiece of this great barn of a place is a 120-foot pewter bar, set among sofas and acres of tables.

Live jazz on Monday nights and DJ suites Thursday to Sunday from 20.00 are the modern manifestations of its musical tradition, with the walls of the dance floor acting as home to exhibitions of modern art and photography.

The place offers itself as a venue for photo shoots and fashion shows too, so it is OK to lean back and stare at the huge pale wooden plank-like beams that stretch forever across the expanse of ceiling. People will just assume you are posing.

This is the only – or should that be first – pub in the UK for the hugely successful Belgian independent brewery, Duvel Moortgat. Although this is very much an experiment to feel the British waters, there is no timidity here. They even have WiFi.

To refer to the food (Sat 11.00–21.00; Sun 11.00–18.00; others 11.00–16.00 & 17.30–22.00) as bar snacks is unfair. The eggs come Benedict, Ranchero, Florentine or Royale and the salads are even more lateral.

Beers are mainly from Duvel Moortgat and friends, so there are Bel Pils, Steendonk wheat beer, the excellent Maredsous range of abbey beers, Bernard from the Czech Republic, plus Pietra and Colomba from Corsica.

Their flagship beer is the world famous Duvel (literally 'Devil'), a deceptively drinkable beer given its 8.5% alcohol content. The bar staff are trained to pour this straw-coloured strong ale, which may throw a light sediment and should sport a rocky white head.

Bavarian Beerhouse

190 City Road EC1V 2QH
T 020 7608 0925
www.bavarian-beerhouse.co.uk
Old Street
Fri & Sat 12.00–01.00
others 12.00–22.00
Erdinger Weissbier Dunkel (5.6%)
Erdinger Weissbräu GmbH, Erding, Germany

"The UK's only authentic German-Bavarian restaurant" can only seat 300 so is a minnow in Bavarian terms. But what does size matter when you have kitsch.

The main beer hall has refectory-style long tables with benches and table service by *Dirndl*-clad *mädchener*. A bright orange cuckoo clock is fixed to a wall of plastic grass, as are fake stags' heads and adverts for German beer. And if you think that is odd, try the Ski Hut.

A bit more pan-Teutonic than the real deal, the Bavarian Beerhouse is nonetheless a great ambassador for German beer. And sausage.

Tiny grilled *Nürnburgers* come on a bed of cabbage with a large *pretzel*. Munich *weisswurst* (white sausages) come immersed in steaming herbal water with printed instructions on how to skin them gracefully. Alternatively they have real black goulash, pork shank or *schnitzel*, with dumplings, noodles and *sauerkraut*.

Pils comes from Warsteiner and there is Küppers Kölsch too, with Munich beers from Paulaner, Hacker-Schorr and Löwenbräu, in litre-sized Steins if you must.

At the outer reaches of the Munich S-Bahn system, and a clever place to stay if you ever visit the Oktoberfest, is the pleasant town of Erding, home to the Erdinger brewery, whose world-renowned wheat beers get a banana character from the yeast used in their fermentation.

Dunkel Weiss (literally 'dark white') has a roasted malt body and is unusually refreshing for a wheat beer.

Betjeman Arms

St Pancras International, Pancras Road NW1 2QP
T 020 7923 5440
www.geronimo-inns.co.uk/thebetjemanarms
Kings Cross or Euston Square
Sat 08.30–23.00; Sun 08.30–22.30
others 07.30–23.00
Betjeman Ale (4.0%) – a.k.a. **Cornish Coaster**
Sharp's Brewery Ltd., Rock, Cornwall

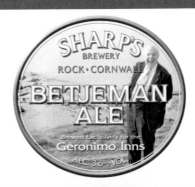

We are taking a risk by including this brand new pub but as the 'First and Last' pub in England for travellers using the Eurostar trains from Paris and Brussels, we hope it will earn its inclusion.

Originally opened in 1868, St Pancras was the grandest of the three mainline rail terminals on Euston Road. When constructed it was an architectural marvel of its age – its main train shed the largest single-span structure ever built.

This ancient and modern pub is on the upper level of the station, next to 'The Meeting Place', a nine-metre-high statue of a couple in a romantic clinch. Not all of its drinking and dining areas were open by the time we went to press but its gastro-pub lampshades probably speak volumes about its direction of travel.

Food is served all day, starting with a full English breakfast and following on with calves liver & bacon, bubble & squeak with a soft-poached egg, or fish & chips with, er, 'crushed peas'.

It is named after conservationist poet Sir John Betjeman, who fought successfully to save this most cathedral-like of stations from demolition in the 1960s.

Betjeman is buried at the tiny church of St Enodoc, near Rock, at the mouth of the river Camel in north Cornwall. It is fitting that the beer given his name is one from the village's own brewery.

Betsey Trotwood

56 Farringdon Road EC1R 3BL
T 020 7253 4285
www.thebetsey.com

Farringdon

CLOSED SUNDAY; Fri & Sat 12.00–01.00
others 12.00–24.00

Bishops Finger (5.0%)

Shepherd Neame, Faversham, Kent

On an island created by streets, opposite the offices of the Guardian newspaper, this nice little pub was built in 1865 on top of the world's first ever underground railway – the four-mile stretch between Farringdon and Paddington, which had been completed in 1863. Hence its rumble.

The recently renovated ground floor is now a single wooden-floored room with a long ecclesiastical bench down one side, a ceiling with handsome light fittings and potted palms dotted throughout. The tables have fresh flowers by day and candles in the evening.

Upstairs is the elegant Acoustic Room bar and assembly room, which can be privately hired when it is not hosting acoustic gigs, comedy or poetry nights.

Downstairs is the Basement Venue, also known as London's cosiest, which although small (capacity 60) has a full PA rig and stage lighting. Keane, Magic Numbers and Kate Nash have all played here.

The Betsey is a tied house owned by the independent Kentish brewers Shepherd Neame. It stocks three of their real ales on tap, including one seasonal offering. A good range of homemade food (Mon–Fri 12.00–15.00; 18.00–21.00) is displayed on the blackboard.

A Bishops Finger is an unusual finger-shaped signpost still found in Kent, which once pointed pilgrims on their way to Canterbury.

The 'Kentish Strong Ale' known as Bishops Finger was first brewed in 1958 to celebrate the lifting of malt rationing after the war that had ended thirteen years earlier. Originally a bottled beer, it was introduced in cask form in 1989. It is produced with locally grown hops and has a fruity but fully rounded flavour.

Tavistock Hotel (basement), Bedford Way WC1H 9EU

T 020 7183 1979
www.bloomsburybowling.com

⊖ Russell Square

🕐 Sun 13.00–24.00; Fri & Sat 12.00–03.00

others 12.00–02.00

🍾 **Bernard Dark** (5.7%)

Pivovar Bernard, Humpolec, Czech Republic

And now for something a little different. This Fifties style ten pin bowling alley and bar is, we believe, unique in London.

Situated below the Tavistock Hotel, its horseshoe-shaped bar is constructed using eighty-year-old cherry maple wood that 'once graced the legendary Lucky Lanes in New York'. Unquestionably stylish, the retro chic look is offset by a nod in the direction of modernity at ceiling level, with exposed pipe and duct-work.

This is a working bowling alley but don't feel obliged. There is plenty of room to people watch from one of the high stools – sit on it and swivel. There are eight lanes for hire in the public bit and a five lane private hire in the Kingpin Suite.

The bar staff are friendly and the service is good. The food menu revolves around classic American burgers and other dishes. Avoid the huge nachos if you are planning on a main meal too – you might end up rolling down the alley yourself.

It is a sign of the times that a popular venue like this must have fine beers. The useful list includes Bitburger and Bernard lagers plus Meantime Pale Ale on draught, plus Gaffel Kölsch, Erdinger Dunkel Weiss and a handful of British beers in the bottle.

Our favourite is the rarely found Bernard Dark, an unpasteurised brew that comes in a stoppered bottle. Brewed in the Moravian highlands of the Czech Republic, it is a strong dark lager made with five types of malt. It is pleasantly bitter with roasted malt, coffee and chocolate in there somewhere.

68 Clapham Manor Street sw4 6dz

T 020 7498 1799

www.breadandrosespub.com

Clapham North & Clapham Common

Fri & Sat 12.00–00.30; Mon & Tue 17.00–11.30
others 12.00–11.30 (11.00 Sun)

Stiegl Bier (4.9%)

Stieglbrauerei zu Salzburg, Salzburg, Austria

Bread & Roses takes its name from a slogan adopted by striking textile workers in Massachusetts in 1912.

It is run by the Workers' Beer Company, which began by supplying volunteers to run beer tents at events such as Glastonbury and now promotes large UK music festivals in its own right, raising money 'to campaign for a better quality of life for working people.'

Hidden down one of the residential streets off Clapham High Street, it is housed in a three-storey Georgian listed building with railings and an outside drinking terrace at the front. Inside is minimalist and modern, with a bright conservatory at the rear.

The Company's first pub brings a lot of festival spirit with it, hosting live music and comedy nights, plus that old revolutionary favourite, Monday chess night.

The food (Tue–Sat 18.00–21.30, Wed–Sun 12.00–15.00, 16.00 Sat) comes from the Observer Life & Style school of cooking with lots of rustic Portuguese bread, home-made *hummus*, black bean veggie burger, red snapper and Cuban beef stew, plus lunchtime *panini* and Sunday roasts.

From an above average and ever changing beer list we have chosen one of Austria's leading independently brewed lagers, Stiegl Bier, which does all the things that a proper blond lager should do.

Bricklayers

31 Waterman Street sw15 1DD

T 020 8789 0222

www.bricklayers-arms.co.uk

⊖ Putney Bridge

⏰ Sun 12.00–22.30

others 12.00–23.00

▥ **Timothy Taylor's Dark Mild** (3.5%)

⊞ Timothy Taylor & Co, Keighley, West Yorkshire

The Bricklayers is a survivor. Situated in a back street close to Putney Bridge, the present building began life in 1826 as the Watermans Arms, though it was raised on the site of an old coach house.

Carrying the flag as Putney's oldest pub it has had a chequered career. It had managed to retain a lot of early internal features including some superb snob screens until the 1990s but was eventually closed down in 2002 and given over to residential use.

That seemed to be end of its working life but remarkably it was re-opened to the public in 2005 and since then has gone from strength to strength, being awarded the accolade of CAMRA's Greater London Pub of the Year in 2007.

This is everything a new-fangled old pub ought to be. The friendly, relaxed, lived-in feel comes from a good mix of local trade. Bar skittles is played. They have regular beer festivals featuring the best of beers from northern breweries.

The absence of a working kitchen has not stopped it from serving food. An outside catering company takes orders and guarantees delivery to your table in 45 minutes.

There is a constant stream of guest beers but true to its northern connection the Bricklayers has an excellent relationship with the outstanding Yorkshire brewery Timothy Taylor's. Uniquely in London they carry their full range of championship-winning beers.

Our featured beer is the Dark Mild. Good mild ale has been difficult to find in the capital for decades, since the heavier industries moved out to the provinces. This one has fruit and malt on the aroma, caramel and hops on the palate and a beautiful dry finish. Light but very satisfying

218 Tower Bridge Road SE1 2UP

T 020 7407 5818

⊖ Tower Hill & London Bridge

🕐 Thu–Sun 11.30–24.00
others 11.30–23.30

▥ **Adnams Bitter** (3.7%)

⊞ Adnams plc, Southwold, Suffolk

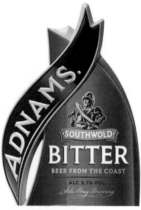

Heading for the Suffolk Coast is a favourite weekend activity of many Londoners, with Adnams brewery of Southwold providing one of the main incentives to be there.

Now the brewery has come to London, opening its first tied house in the capital, on the approach road to the south side of Tower Bridge, with a rear entrance in Horselydown Lane.

The bar fascia is decorated in the royal blue of Adnams livery. The downstairs bar is fitted out in a modern style complete with light wooden floors, tables and taupe suede fabric seats.

There is an upstairs dining area, which is also available for functions. There is also an eating area downstairs, down one wall of the ground floor bar.

Food leans to the 'gourmet' and offers amongst others honey-glazed duck breast and lentils and chicken liver and brandy parfait with red onion jam and toast. Even the cheese and tomato sarnies are posh, the bread being an organic baguette and the cheese smoked on applewood.

Adnams are not just brewers. They also run one of the most reliable wine importing businesses in Britain, so the wine list is well above average for a beer bar.

All of Adnams' beers are available on handpull, including the seasonal varieties. However, in deference to the simplicity that made them famous among beer lovers, why not try their most popular and multi-award winning Bitter – exactly the sort of low-strength, high calibre, distinctive thirst quencher that the British do so well.

Bünker Bierhall

41 Earlham Street WC2H 9LX
T 020 7240 0606
www.bunkerbar.com
Covent Garden
Sun 12.00–22.30
others 12.00–24.00
Freedom Dark Lager (4.7%)
Freedom Brewery, Abbots Bromley, Staffordshire

ABV 4.7%
Organic Certification UK5
Vegan
FREEDOM
Exceptional when served at 2°
ORGANIC DARK LAGER

It seems appropriate that Covent Garden should have an underground brewery hidden away somewhere. This is it.

Even more appropriately, it is found in the Seven Dials – a collection of streets designed for well-to-do 18th century Londoners that fell quickly into disrepute, causing Dickens to observe, "It is evident whatever there may be a lack of in the Dials, there is no lack of money for drink."

The exterior is a brick arch affair from which steps lead down to a huge, cavernous underground room with a bar down its longest side. Vaulted brick ceilings are held up by riveted ceiling joists and silver pillars. The modern industrial design is

completed by the concrete and wood flooring, with ducting and venting on show.

A side area with large refectory-style tables and benches acts as a restaurant space with reservations from 19.00 onwards. Home-made pies – chicken & ham, smoked haddock & leek and steak & Soho Red – are served with mash and beans.

It attracts a younger crowd but not exclusively so. Music is played, there is a small dance floor and they have regular 'beach parties'.

At the far end the bar's own microbrewery is on display. Beers for the Freedom brewery, called Soho Red and Freedom Pilsener are brewed on site at the Bunker by Master Brewer Ian Ward, to the rules of the sadly defunct *Reinheitsgebot* German purity law of 1564, with no adjuncts or additives used in production.

This organic dark lager is brewed at the parent company's brewhouse in the Midlands.

Carpenter's Arms

73 Cheshire Street E2 6EG

T 020 7739 6342

www.carpentersarmsfreehouse.com

Bethnal Green

Fri & Sat 12.00–00.30

others 12.00–23.30

Dorothy Goodbody's Country Ale (6.0%)

Wye Valley Brewery, Stoke Lacy, Herefordshire

Nestled on a corner of a street among the still operational warehouses and textile wholesalers of this working area of inner East London, this surprisingly beautiful, almost perfect little pub is a tribute to the power of the refit.

Its handsome frontage is illuminated at night by candles placed in storm lanterns in the windows. Inside is a forest of wood – floors, tables, chairs and benches, panelled walls – brightened by natural light from huge windows.

How it has avoided being turned into fashionable apartments we have no idea but like to think it has had nothing to do with the family that used to own it. Rumour has it that the Kray twins liked it so much that in 1967 they bought it for their mum – hence the mirror displaying tasteful portraits of Ronnie and Reggie, Elvis-style.

The simple but elegant interior has fresh flowers, candelabra and chandeliers. A tiny back room closes, ominously, by way of a lockable prison-style barred gate. A display of saws and hammers hark back to the trade tools of the eponymous Carpenters of the pubs name.

A new kitchen has been installed so food is set to expand.

The impressive, not to say bewildering list of beers is displayed on a huge blackboard opposite the front door. You will often find beers from the Brooklyn brewery in New York or from Little Creatures in Freemantle, Western Australia.

Our chosen beer comes from the excellent Wye Valley brewery in rural Herefordshire. Its Dorothy Goodbody range is pretty impressive. The Country Ale is a ruby-coloured ale, sweet, malt-laden and hearty.

Cask & Glass

39 Palace Street SW1E 5HN
T 020 7834 7630
www.shepherd-neame.co.uk/pubs/pubs.php/caskandglass_
Victoria
CLOSED SUNDAY; Sat 12.00–20.00
others 11.00–23.00
Shepherd Neame Kent's Best (4.1%)
Shepherd Neame, Faversham, Kent

Dwarfed by the butt-ugly high rise offices of Westminster City Council and other developments, this sweet little pub nestles on Palace Road, not far from the Royal Mews at Buckingham Palace.

This is an attractive setting on a street corner, festooned with flower baskets and flanked by huge cordyline palms through which you must fight your way to get inside.

Reputed to be the smallest pub in Westminster, its bijou interior is unsuitable for cat-swinging and has a traditional feel from the dark panelled walls, red carpets and heavy heraldic curtains. There is brown buttoned-back banquette seating round its edge, and stools.

The walls are decorated with mock-gilt mirrors and black and white pictures of people doing things in a brewery. This turns out to Shepherd Neame's brewery in Faversham in Kent, which they claim is the oldest brewery in continuous production in the UK.

Lunch is served on weekdays only. The small TV screen in the corner comes into its own on Saturday afternoons when a small but keen horse-racing fraternity gathers.

There are four Shepherd Neame beers on handpull here, including Kent's Best, a copper-coloured bitter ale made with Kentish hops from near the brewery. It has a light malty aroma and a dry, hoppy taste.

26 Furnival Street EC4A 1JS

T 020 7405 5470

Chancery Lane

CLOSED SATURDAY & SUNDAY
others 11.00–23.00

Red Car Best Bitter (3.9%) – a.k.a. **Three Point Nine**

Nethergate Brewery Co., Pentlow, Essex

Guesstimating the future prices of cocoa butter and selenium dioxide is vitally important and thirsty work. Which probably explains why this simple little corner pub down a narrow street off High Holborn is always crammed with rehydrating suits.

Its forbidding dark black frontage, incorporating a plaque from 1901, is relieved by copious foliage in season. Its single small room has bare wooden floorboards, dark wood panelling and a red ceiling.

In the evening there are welcoming candles in the huge windows that are its main feature. Seating is mainly tall drinking perches and high bar stools, with not a Chesterfield sofa in sight.

Food (12.00–15.00) is simple, with roasts, doorsteps and toasties. An upstairs room used for overspill on Fridays is also available for hire at other times.

The beer is what brings people to this little City oasis. Eight handpulls draw an ever changing array of guest ales from the cellar including many from smaller microbreweries, from which Nethergate brewery secures a permanent presence by supplying the house beer.

Red Car Best Bitter is, we think, the brewery's Three Point Nine rebadged – a copper-coloured, fruity best bitter with an earthy, malty aroma.

Charles Lamb

16 Elia Street N1 8DE
T 020 7837 5040
www.thecharleslambpub.com
Angel
Sun 12.00–22.30; Mon & Tue 16.00–23.00
others 12.00–23.00
Anchor Steam Liberty Ale (5.9%)
Anchor Steam Brewery, San Francisco, USA

This two-roomed corner pub in is named after the early 19th century writer, who lived nearby. The street is named after, *Essays of Elia*, his 1823 *magnum opus*.

It has a light, modern feel with pale wood floors and furnishings. One of several ceramic cockerels stands on the bar holding a pile of light snacks. In the smaller side room hang maps of London, New York, France and elsewhere.

Formal painted wooden signs warn customers not to feed Mascha, the pub's Staffordshire bull terrier, who wears neck scarves, has her own pitch on MySpace and is happy to meet anyone who is not a cat.

The food (Mon–Wed 18.00–21.00; Thu–Sat 12.30–15.00 & 18.00–21.00; Sun 13.00–18.00) is mouth-wateringly excellent. Try sweet potato squash & orange soup, crab chilli & fennel tart, or lamb *merguez* with puy lentils & *crème fraîche*. They claim not be a gastro pub as they do not take bookings, so you could stick with pickled eggs.

Its eclectic beer list has more American ales than most, with several from Anchor Steam. This traditional old brewery was rescued from closure in the late 1960's by Fritz Maytag, an unwitting champion of craft brewing in the US, who famously intervened because he 'just liked the place'.

Their Liberty Ale was first brewed in 1975 to commemorate the bicentennial of Paul Revere's famous ride. Its rich body and distinctively American hopping has remained popular ever since.

Cittie of Yorke

22 High Holborn WC1V 6BS
T 020 7242 7670
Holborn
CLOSED SUNDAY; Sat 12.00–23.00
others 11.30–23.00
Sam Smith Oatmeal Stout (5.0%)
Samuel Smith Old Brewery, Tadcaster, North Yorkshire

There has been a pub here at the gates to the old City of London for several hundred years. The current incarnation is actually far newer than it looks, being a supreme example of 'Brewers' Tudor', the early 20th century fad for making pubs look respectable by creating timber-framed fantasy buildings.

The frontage is all panelled doors and mullioned windows. You enter down an enclosed passageway. To the left is a relatively restrained square front bar with the odd heraldic drape, dark panelling and heavy light fittings. The real (mock) deal is straight ahead.

The church-sized main room has a pitched beam black and white ceiling above a great hall with an expanse of wooden flooring with a curious stand-alone, three-cornered iron stove and giant wooden barrels on shelves above the bar.

Above, a 'minstrels' gallery' is held up by wooden arches that create spaces for a dozen snug, four-seater booths, each adorned with a wrought iron portcullis. To appreciate this place's full grandeur try to catch it just as it opens. There are few other times when it is quiet.

The independent Yorkshire brewery, Sam Smith's, is renowned in London for low prices and own-brand drinks behind the bar. There are no big brand spirits or soft drinks here. Nor music since the Performing Rights levy was introduced.

As other brewers were rising to the challenge of the real ale revival, Sam's decided to develop a range of fine bottled ales instead, aimed at the US market.

Sam Smith's Oatmeal Stout is a smooth, creamy, sweetish black beer with coffee and chocolate aromas, brewed with oats in the mash.

Cove

The Piazza WC2E 8RB
T 020 7836 7880
www.coventgardenlife.com/places.asp?PlaceID=332
Covent Garden
Sun 12.00–22.30
others 11.00–23.00
Skinner's Betty Stogs Bitter (4.0%)
Skinner's Brewing Co, Truro, Cornwall

If you can't afford to take the seven hundred mile round trip to the tip of Cornwall, come to Covent Garden and get the cartoon version.

Above the West Cornwall Pasty Company and accessed through its shop, narrow stairs lead to a loosely themed warren that conflates the feel of a tin mine with the whiff of seafaring.

Plank and stone flooring, rough-painted walls, heavy timbers, unvarnished wooden furnishings, a bar in the shape of a ship, rope swags, lifebuoy rings, wooden floats, red and green nautical lights and lobster pots – you get the drift?

Beyond is a narrow walkway leading to a couple of smaller areas, recessed down a few stairs. Its sizeable terrace has a great view over the Piazza, where a cacophony of top quality licensed street entertainers perform their stuff.

The food chimes with the London Cornish theme, as pasties come with ten different fillings from the shop below.

The breweries of the county-cum-nation state provide the ales too. Skinner's is based in the capital, Truro, and enjoys an excellent local reputation. Betty Stogs is a solid, copper-coloured bitter with a fine balance of malt, hop and fruity flavours.

Ms Stogs was a hapless, neglectful wife and mother of legend, who mislaid her baby, only to find it returned by piskies – the Little People, Cornwall style.
Or at least that was what she told the child protection people.

Crown & Sceptre

26–27 Foley St w1w 6ds

T 020 7307 9971

Oxford Circus

Sun 12.00–22.30
others 12.00–23.00

Schneider Weisse (5.4%)

Privatbrauerei G Schneider & Sohn,
Kelheim, Germany

The large crown and sceptre fashioned into the red brick wall above the door of this pretty corner pub in Fitzrovia would make renaming it an expensive affair.

Inside a number of other original features have been retained including a fine moulded ceiling and a couple of imposing Corinthian columns holding it up across the expanse of the large, open square-ish main room. The floor is wooden of course and the chairs and stools are elegantly mismatched.

There is a small side area similarly furnished with the addition of sofa-like comfy seating.

Huge windows from ceiling to seat level create a light open space by day, while at night the window ledges are sprinkled with myriad coloured glass tea-light holders tempting in passers by. A stuffed wild boar's head and antler light nod in the direction of 19th century tastes in interior fittings.

The menu darts all over the place, from *wasabi* pea bar snacks to *tapas* and *nachos* for two, via rolls like fish finger & lime mayo, to 'Big Food' like burger & chips or a grass-fed sirloin steak. Veggies get wild mushroom risotto with asparagus or char-grilled *haloumi* and roasted vegetable with *couscous*.

The beer range is eclectic too, with Czech Budvar Dark plus Belgian Liefmans Frambozen and Maredsous Blond on tap. We have gone instead for an excellent German wheat beer from a large family-owned brewery near Munich.

Schneider Weisse is darker than the average wheat beer, with a yeasty aroma followed by lemon and clove flavours before a dry, faintly sour finish.

Crown Tavern

43 Clerkenwell Green EC1R 0EG
T 020 7253 4973
→ Farringdon
Fri & Sat 12.00–01.00
others 12.00–24.00
Kriek 100% Lambic Cantillon (5.0%)
Brasserie Cantillon, Brussels, Belgium

CANTILLON

Kriek 100% Lambic

Clerkenwell Green is a highly fashionable address right now and this huge pub and its terrace are right on it.

The several rooms include a comfortable lounge at the back with a wooden floor and panelling plus dark red walls. A retro feel nods to the ghastly 70s with birdcage-style lamps, low tables, cube stools, Chesterfield, sofas and cushions all in the brown, orange and beige palette of the decade.

In the evening it is dimly lit and atmospheric, becoming an attractive haunt for students, with music that varies from moody to noisy.

A man in the gentlemen's lavatory squirts your hands with liquid soap then hands you a paper towel, whether you want one or not. We are unsure whether this is an intended feature of the pub, or just an enthusiastic local.

The real ales on offer include Adnams' Bitter and Timothy Taylor's Landlord with guests, alongside a well-above-average selection of European draughts. There is also a large selection of quality bottled beers, particularly from the US, Germany and Belgium.

Our featured beer is the rare and challenging Cantillon Kriek. This is a cherry beer – *kriek* meaning cherry in old Dutch – made by steeping whole fruit in oak casks of lambic, a beer fermented using naturally occurring air-borne yeast.

Approach this drink as a beer and you may well not get it. On the other hand if you start by imagining it is like a traditional dry cider or even Champagne slowly but surely the part of your brain that interprets what your taste buds are telling you will work it out.

And once you work it out, you will never look on beer using the same narrow parameters again.

Czech and Slovak Club

74 West End Lane NW6 2LX
T 020 7372 5251
www.czechandslovakclub.co.uk
West Hampstead
Sat & Sun 12.00–23.00
others 17.00–23.00
Budweiser Budvar Premium Lager (5.0%)
Budějovický Budvar, České Budějovice, Czech Republic

ORIGINAL
Budweiser Budvar

This is not a theme bar, it is the real thing. Little has changed to the fabric of this club since it was opened shortly after the Second World War by a group of Czechoslovakian ex-pats.

In its brief history it has reflected the massive political changes 'back home'. Soviet-style communism stuttered briefly in the Prague Spring of 1968 before the return of the occupying army, eventually removed in the Velvet Revolution of 1989. The separation of Slovakia from the Czech Republic was unusually amicable, the rise of capitalism culminating in the two nations eventually joining the EU and the Euro.

The club is housed in a large detached house set back from the road near West Hampstead tube station. The illuminated Pilsner Urquell sign and faintly comic mannequin chef are easily missed.

Each room has an allocated use. The bar and meeting rooms all lead off a central hallway. On the right is the restaurant (opening time to 22.30) with a huge choice of Czechoslovak favourites including interesting things done with carp, goose, pork and dumplings.

Second on the left brings you to a bar straight out of 1960s Prague, with melamine tables and black squishy plastic mock tiles lining the lower walls. The TV in the corner has all the latest news from Bratislava.

The beer list includes Bernard Dark but in a place like this you just have to drink draught Budvar from České Budějovice, the southern Bohemian town known in German as Budweis.

Budweiser Budvar is a crisp and clean tasting golden lager with a dense white head, an aroma of biscuit and a long taste of malt and grain.

Dog & Duck

18 Bateman Street W1D 3AJ
T 020 7494 0697
➤ Tottenham Court Road
🕒 Sun 12.00–23.30; Fri & Sat 11.00–23.30
others 11.00–23.00
🍺 **Timothy Taylor's Landlord (4.3%)**
🍻 Timothy Taylor & Co, Keighley, West Yorkshire

We do not know whether this is the original Dog & Duck much loved of cartoonists and columnists over the years but its lengthy pedigree and position in the heart of Soho suggests it could be.

The original pub was built in 1734 on land owned by the Duke of Monmouth. The menu claims that Soho was then hunting grounds, its name derived from 'so-ho', an old hunting call.
[Ed: my grandma used to claim that oysters were wrinkly because they were cooked in their shells but that did not make it true.]

The current building dates from 1897, the decade when pub design was in its pomp. Its handsome exterior corners Frith Street.

Its downstairs bar is tiny and narrow with a small snug attached. The late Victorian decoration is ornate and elaborate. The walls are a riot of colourful glazed tiles, gilt and painted advertising mirrors, the ceiling deep red and embossed. The dog and his duck appear in a repeating pattern on the lower tiled part of the wall opposite the bar.

Upstairs the George Orwell Bar & Dining Room is dedicated to the novelist who used this pub in his journalistic days. A cosy little room with nice wood panelled walls and its own bar, it affords a close up view of the two handsome pub signs, in sky blue and gold, depicting dog in hot pursuit of duck.

Food here (12.00–21.00) is big on sausages.

Famously, when Madonna visited this little gem she opted for a pint of Timothy Taylor's Landlord. So should you. This multi-award winning best bitter has been brewed since 1953 and is now this Yorkshire brewery's flagship ale. A copper-coloured classic with a clever aromatic hop character and satisfying drinkability.

Doric Arch

1 Eversholt Street NW1 1DN

T 020 7388 2221

⊖ Euston

🕐 Sun 12.00–22.30
others 11.00–23.00

🍺 Hop Back Summer Lightning (5.0%)

⊞ Hop Back Brewery, Downton, Wiltshire

From the time of its construction in 1838 until the height of Lord Beeching's powers in 1962, Euston Station had as its main entrance a 70 foot high neo-classical pillared gateway in solid stone.

Rumour has it that 4000 tons of original arch rubble has been located in the River Lea and that it is to be reconstructed as part of the station's redevelopment. Hence the pub's recent change of name from the Head of Steam. Resurgam!

This part of Euston Road is the city's biggest transport hub, with three railway terminals, a bus station and numerous tube stations. This first floor bar in a modern building has a large main room with a wooden floor and a raised area with acorn-topped wooden balustrades that overlook the bus station.

It is decorated with railway memorabilia such as enamel station signs, train number plates and delightful old travel posters. You can tell you are in the UK though, as the locked toilet is protected by a four digit code, which the bar staff will delight in hollering at you from a distance.

Food (Mon–Fri 12.30–15.00 & 16.00–20.30; Sat & Sun 12.00–17.00) is standard pub grub. The TV majors on sport but this still makes a better place to linger between trains or buses than other waiting rooms.

This is a Fullers pub that serves many guest beers. One is now a permanent resident.

Hop Back's Summer Lightning was first brewed in the late 1980s and is the original British 'golden ale'. Initially summer only it is now year-round. Its straw colour, strong hop and citric notes are much imitated but rarely bettered.

Dove

24 Broadway Market E8 4QJ

T 020 7275 7617

www.belgianbars.com

➜ Bethnal Green

⇌ London Fields & Cambridge Heath

☽ Fri & Sat 12.00–01.00

others 12.00–23.00

Rochefort 8 (9.2%)

▐ Brasserie de l'Abbaye Notre Dame de Saint Rémy, Rochefort, Belgium

Broadway Market is undergoing a revival of fortunes and Saturdays (09.00–17.00) sees a bustling farmers' market outside this fine corner pub.

The front room is light and airy, with an imitation of Michelangelo's 'Creation of Adam' on its ceiling – not as grand as in the Sistine Chapel but not bad for Hackney. The rest of the inside is wood from the floors and balustrades to the impressive and unusual panelled walls.

Rooms of one sort or another branch off everywhere. Bare wood tables are candle-lit by night. Framed prints hang on the walls. The dark wood, low ceilings and absence of natural light give the back room a snug, cosy feel.

You can eat anywhere inside (Thu–Sun 12.00–22.00, 23.00 Fri & Sat; others 12.00–15.00 & 18.00–22.00). Daily specials may include venison casserole, whole roast sea bass, or pan-fried pheasant breast. Chips are served by the tumbler.

There is a sister pub in Clerkenwell (Jerusalem Passage) called the Dovetail.

Despite its classically English appearance and four cask ales, what stands out is the list of Belgian beers, which include a number of challenging beers beyond the well-known brands.

Belgium is home to six of the world's seven Trappist breweries, where brewing is overseen by Trappist fathers. None come more highly recommended than the beers from the abbey at Rochefort. Their most famous brew is Rochefort 8, a deep, dark, full luscious ale that should be sipped contemplatively.

30 St Peters Street N1 8JT

T 020 7359 9450

www.dukeorganic.co.uk/duke.html

⊖ Angel

🕐 Sun 12.00–22.30

others 12.00–23.00

St Peters Organic Best Bitter (4.1%)

St Peters Brewery, Co., St. Peter South Elmham, Suffolk

S Peter's
Brewery
ORGANIC
BEST BITTER

ALC. 4.1% VOL.
Organic Certification UK5

"Britain's first and only certified organic pub" opened in 1998 and has been hitting eco-milestones ever since. Organic soaps arrived in 1998, while 1999 saw it host the launch of organic tampons, still available in the Ladies' loo.

Organic palm oil candles grace the dining room tables that populate the open, airy, square main room. Bare wooden floors with a welter of mismatched wooden chairs have worn in over the years.

The side room and conservatory are set up for diners and all ingredients are, of course, sourced from organic suppliers. Freshness dictates that the menu for lunch (daily 12.30–15.00, 15.30 Sat & Sun) and dinner (18.30–22.30, 22.00 Sun) changes sometimes on an hourly basis – consult the blackboard.

They stock over 40 organic wines and a great range of Fair Trade teas.

The pub is Soil Association Certified, as is Pitfield Brewery, which supplies their own-brand organic draught bitter, SB. You will also find Britain's first organic draught lager from Freedom Brewery – another in favour with the Soil Association – created originally for this pub.

St. Peter's Brewery from deep in rural Suffolk gets the nod too, supplying its Organic Best Bitter on handpull. Made from Chariot malted barley and Goldings hops, the result is a light tawny, full-bodied, best bitter that is highly drinkable.

Eagle Ale House

104 Chatham Road SW11 6HG

T 020 7228 2328

⇌ Clapham Junction

☽ Sun 12.00–22.30

others 12.00–23.00

▌ **British Bulldog BB** (4.3%)

⊟ Westerham Brewery Co., Crookham, Kent

Northcote Road in Wandsworth, sat between the two commons of Wandsworth and Clapham, is nowadays clogged with so many outlets for cocktails, cappuccino and Côte du Rhone that the survival of this unreconstructed ale house comes as an increasingly unlikely relief.

The Eagle is a down-to-earth boozer, its feet set firmly in a culture that locally predated the new insurgents by centuries. Maintaining a strong pub tradition does not mean becoming dilapidated though and the place has been going through a major spruce up recently.

Free of tie and fiercely independent, it has featured over 5,000 different guest beers over the years, a fair proportion coming from smaller, newer independent breweries.

An impressive beer festival is run every March in the huge, heated marquee in the walled garden behind, which spends the rest of the year as a smoking area. There is also a terrace at the front in the warmer weather, with sun shades.

Although one of its biggest pulling points is the ever-changing roster of quality real ales, one beer remains throughout. Westerham Brewery only started life in 2004 but they have been quick to expand, currently supplying over 100 outlets in Kent and clearly intent on getting more accounts in London.

British Bulldog, or BB, is a traditional best bitter brewed with Kentish hops. It is a balanced beer with prominent malt and fruit character with distinct hop notes.

40–41 Essex St WC2R 3JE

T 020 7353 3120

www.edgarwallacepub.com

⊖ Temple

🕓 CLOSED SATURDAY & SUNDAY; Mon–Fri 11.00–23.00

▥ **Edgar's Pale Ale EPA** (3.5%) – a.k.a. **Nethergate IPA**

⊞ Nethergate Brewery Co., Pentlow, Essex

Between the Royal Courts of Justice on the Strand and the Victoria Embankment lies the Temple, founded by the Knights Templar in 1160, stolen and sold back to them by Edward II and eventually nicked again by Henry VIII in 1540. It has been the heartland of British justice for over 500 years.

Built as the Essex Head at the north edge of the Temple in 1777, this pub soon became the place where the ageing and infirm Dr Samuel Johnson held court. 200 years later, it was renamed after an author of different talents, Edgar Wallace (1875–1932), prolific crime writer, inventor of the thriller and co-creator of King Kong.

Its forbidding presence owes much to its solid black walls and small-paned portcullis windows, conjuring up an image of Victorian prisons. However inside the main square room manages a much lighter feel.

The menu is clearly aimed at one-plate diners, with an all day breakfast, beer battered cod, grilled *haloumi* and chicken *schnitzel* among others. The upstairs function room opens to all for lunch (12.00–15.00).

A vast array of English ales is normally on handpull, the permanent fixtures of which are Adnams Bitter and Nethergate IPA, sold as Edgar Wallace Pale Ale (EPA). Founded in the Suffolk village of Clare in 1986, Nethergate Brewery's success forced them to move to larger premises in nearby Pentlow in 2006.

Edgar's Pale Ale EPA is an amber-coloured session beer which drinks above its weight. The brewery's other beers are appearing more frequently in the capital and are well worth searching out.

Fifth View

203–206 Piccadilly W1J 9LE
T 020 7851 2433
www.5thview.co.uk
➔ Piccadilly Circus
☽ Sun 12.00–18.00
others 10.00–22.00
Chimay Grande Réserve (9.0%)
Bières de Chimay, Baileux, Belgium

Doors opening. 5th Floor. Convenient for meeting pals before visiting the Royal Academy, Fortnum & Mason or just doing a spot of shopping in Bond Street, the café on the 5th floor of Europe's largest book store, Waterstone's in Piccadilly, is a delight.

It is a large, airy, comfortable space with picture windows overlooking the London skyline. You can spot the London Eye peeping at you over the rooftops, near to the towers of the Palace of Westminster. A mirrored wall down one side makes the café seem even larger than it is. Fresh flowers and jazz say relax.

Black and steel chairs with small side tables and longer sofas by coffee tables are designed as much for those dining alone with a book as for the early evening *tapas* crowd. For a less formal area a second room is found opposite the lifts.

Food (lunch Mon–Fri 12.00–15.00; brunch Sat & Sun 12.00–16.00; tapas daily 17.00–21.00) is all made on the premises and may include fresh tomato & chorizo soup with warm *focaccia*, sandwiches, salads, cakes and excellent savoury tarts – try the field mushroom, thyme & brie, or smoked salmon with roast fennel & dill.

They do cocktails and have a wine list and all that, but being a classy kind of joint they also have an impressive selection of bottled beers, including this massive offering from the Trappist Abbey of Scourmont, near the market town of Chimay in southern Belgium.

Chimay Grande Réserve is found only in 75cl bottles intended for sharing, like wine, except best poured in a single go to avoid being drowned in its own sediment. Warm the glass gently in your palm to get the most from this deep brown ale, fruity as an over-ripe plum and slightly bitter from roasted malt.

Fish Shop

360–362 St. John Street EC1V 4NR

T 020 7837 1199

www.thefishshop.net

⊖ Angel

⏲ CLOSED MONDAY; Sun 12.00–18.30
others 12.00–15.00; 17.30–23.00

🍾 **Pitfield N1 Wheat Beer** (5.0%)

▦ Pitfield Brewery, North Weald, Essex

London has a number of well scrubbed-up fish restaurants but as far as we are aware this is the only one also offering a top-rate range of bottle-conditioned beers to go alongside.

The smart, black-painted frontage sits opposite the Islington end of Rosebery Avenue, the home of Sadler's Wells Theatre. The place has a crisp, clean feel and the candle lit tables are spread with white linen. Eating areas spread over several floors and onto a front terrace in the summer. There is a narrow bar at the front.

To start try the rock oysters, seared scallops with celeriac *purée* & sauce *vièrge* or grilled split langoustines in Pernod & tarragon butter. Or stick with whelks.

Mains run from cod, chips (hand cut of course) & mushy peas to pan-fried skate stuffed with leek & horseradish with spinach & caperberry sauce, or grilled swordfish with baked tomato, crispy parsnips & basil mascarpone sauce.

Of course they have an extensive wine list – who doesn't? But what a surprise on the beer front – a list that contains helpful and accurate tasting notes, plus advice on finding good beer and food pairings.

Until 2006 the Pitfield Brewery was but a salmon's leap from here, in nearby Pitfield Street. Research by their erstwhile brewer Martyn Cornell enabled them to recreate some stonking beers to original recipes, such as a Porter (from 1850), Imperial Stout (1792), Amber Ale (1830) and India Pale Ale (1837).

Pitfield's N1 Wheat Beer is brewed in the hazy, lightly spiced, Belgian style and goes well with quite a variety of fish dishes. Sweetish, with a touch of the coriander, it has light citrus fruit notes too.

Flea Pit

49 Columbia Road E2 7RG
T 0207 033 99 86
www.thefleapit.com

→ Bethnal Green

CLOSED MONDAY; Sun 10.00–14.00; Sat 12.30–23.00
others 17.30–23.00

Freedom Organic Lager (4.8%)

Freedom Brewery, Abbots Bromley, Staffordshire

ABV 4.8%
Organic Certification UK5

Vegan

Exceptional when served at 2°

FREEDOM
ORGANIC LAGER

This unusual combination of pub and arts venue is near the end of Shoreditch's newly fashionable Colombia Road – long known for its Sunday flower market, opposite a lovely curve of Victorian terrace shops.

It was created by ripping the guts out of a Victorian warehouse, making the Lounge a light, open space. Galvanised industrial ducting, whitewashed brick walls and a khaki ceiling make the dark wood bar and beer shelves look posh. The Pit hosts the events – mainly music, poetry and arts gigs.

Much of the painted wooden floor is taken up with hideous mock leather, velour buttoned 1970s sofas and armchairs, matched with glass topped tables. The effect is topped off by one of those sunburst clocks. It is nice to see these trophies, which once journeyed from fashionable to unmentionable in less than a decade, being acceptable once more. Maybe there is Life on Mars after all.

Soft drinks include freshly squeezed fruit and veg. Vegetarian snacks are available all day (to 22.00).

There is a buying policy for all consumables that favours small producers only. So there are organic spirits and even an eco-friendly Champagne, at a price. This makes creating a beer list quite a challenge. The only draught is Freedom Organic Lager but there is dark Potro from Mexico and loads of Pitfield beers.

Britain's reputation for top quality lagers is as thin as the products themselves. At last one of two better quality brews are nudging in, such as this organic offering – like lager only interesting.

133 Dulwich Road SE24 0NG
T 020 7326 4987
www.florencehernehill.com

≥ Herne Hill
⊖ Brixton
⏱ Fri 11.00–01.30; Sat 10.00–01.30; Sun 10.00–24.00
others 11.00–24.00
▥ Weasel Beer (4.5%)
⊞ Florence Brewpub, Herne Hill, London

WEASEL BEER
BREWED IN HOUSE
FRUITY, FLORAL
LINGERING MOUTH-FEEL,
GOLDEN IN COLOUR
WITH A DISTINCTLY
CITRUS NOSE
4.5% ABV

As London prepares for the 2012 Olympics it is worth noting that the velodrome at Herne Hill, the spiritual home of British cycling, is the only sports facility still in use from London's last Olympics in 1948.

The Florence sits next to Herne Hill station. Its brown-tiled Victorian fascia is almost hidden by newly added black paintwork and the bright red pull-down shades that protect the front windows from the blazing sun of a South London summer, enjoyed full on in the airy conservatory and large outside drinking areas.

Its huge island bar is cooled by a fan straight from a Sydney Greenstreet movie, each a centrepiece of this large brewpub. The brewing installation itself is condemned to a separate room cut off from the bar by glass screens because of rules made up by paranoid catastrophisers in Health & Safety.

Modern British food (Sun to 21.30, others to 22.00) includes old British food such as Colchester oysters with a pint of stout or haddock & chips with mushy peas, plus newer creations like chicken, crayfish & asparagus mash-topped pie. Steaks come from both cows and aubergines.

Despite making their own beers, they stock a load of other people's from round the globe, particularly in bottle.

Weasel is a refreshing, golden, zesty pint with a peach aroma and noticeable splash of grapefruit in its aftertaste.

Foundry

84–86 Great Eastern Street EC2A 3JL

T 020 7739 6900

www.foundry.tv

➔ Old Street

CLOSED MONDAY

Tue–Fri 16.30–23.00; Sat 14.30–23.00; Sun 14.30–22.30

Pitfield Eco Warrior (4.5%)

Pitfield Brewery, North Weald, Essex

ORGANIC

PITFIELD's

ECO WARRIOR

ORGANICALLY BREWED PALE ALE

ABV 4.5%   50cl

This unique bar nestles at the foot of an ugly old bank building currently sheathed in a grey fabric frontage.

Inside, well, how do you put it? It is not scruffy – that would be flattering. Earthy? Raw? Arty, in an East-Berlin-post-Stasi sort of way?

It is a spaghetti pile of doodles and cartoons, hand-drawn posters, political posturing, concrete flooring, wire swags, antiquated computer screens with video art, red Formica tables and … well, is the gas canister underneath the baby grand piano an art installation or a storage issue?

For survivors of late 1960s student sit-ins or mid 1970s Student Union bars it poses no reality issues – just the spectre of what Alzheimer's might bring in years to come. It might be easier to comprehend if they weren't so friendly. Sadly, they are.

You're a grown-up (probably) so make your own mind up. But not before clocking the 'main bar' and odd little snug that come straight out of middle England in a time when sitcom was king, complete with three piece suite, coffee table and rug.

Not sure whether this bar has already had its fifteen minutes of fame or whether it is yet to come. At least this one does not have beige walls and Chesterfield sofas. It seems to be a rule of thumb that if it is a seriously interesting bar then it stocks beers from Pitfield.

Anyway, try the bottle conditioned Eco Warrior, brewed entirely from organic malt, hops and cane sugar, with a certificate to prove it. Unlike some organic beers, this one is even suitable for vegans. It is a pale golden beer with a fruity sweetness.

43

115 Charterhouse Street EC1M 6AA

T 020 7250 1300

www.foxandanchor.com

Barbican

CLOSED SUNDAY

others 07.00–23.00

Meantime London Porter (6.5%)

Meantime Brewing Co., Greenwich, London

This place's swaggeringly confident website opens with the words, 'The Pub just got chic'. We should hate it but, sadly, it really is very good.

Situated close to the 800-year-old but state-of-the-art Smithfield meat market, it opens early for the traders. Its beautifully preserved late Victorian frontage features mosaics and coloured tiles, with ornate carvings that include two fierce gargoyles lunging above eye level at passers by.

The dark green interior is relieved by wood panelling, mirrored wall dividers, tiling and a nice embossed ceiling. Pleasingly undisturbed by the passage of time, its long, narrow main room widens towards the rear spawning numerous unfeasibly tiny alcoves for diners. Many have only enough space for a table and two chairs.

Ordinarily for Victorian times but unusually for the present day, it has a pewter bar top and often serves its draught ales in pewter tankards with glass bottoms – just in case some nasty press gang slips the King's shilling into your pint and then drags you off to join the Royal Navy on false pretences. Really.

Breakfast (Mon–Fri 08.00–11.00) is fit for a king, even without suggested 'breakfast beers', such as Nethergate Old Growler or St. Peter's Cream Stout, and whether or not you have stayed overnight in one of their six well-appointed bedrooms.

Lunch (daily 12.00–17.00) and dinner (Mon–Sat 17.00–22.00) are described modestly as 'gloriously gastronomic, thankfully local' and include potted beef & piccalilli, Cromer crab, fresh Essex Blackwater oysters and rib of beef on the bone with Yorkshire pudding & roasted bone marrow.

Top quality English and foreign bottled beers abound here but we have chosen Meantime Brewery's Porter in 75cl caged and corked bottles, a black-as-yer-boot hulk of a beer with a superb bittersweet balance – a classic of its kind.

Freemasons

2 Wandsworth Common North Side SW18 2SS

T 020 7326 8580

www.freemasonspub.com

≋ Clapham Junction

🕐 Fri & Sat 12.00–24.00; Sun 12.00–22.30

   Others 12.00–23.00

▥ **Tiger Best Bitter** (4.2%)

✚ Everards Brewery Ltd, Enderby, Leicestershire

This fine gastro-pub is found opposite the northern end of Wandsworth Common, a very long way from the tube station of the same name.

The once grand Victorian building has a prominent semi-circular fascia with portholes at the lower levels and currently sports a striking burgundy colour. Beyond the fine entrance is a new interior with a circular bar matching the front building line, faced in light wood.

Floors and furnishings are wooden except for the obligatory sofas. The overall feel is light and airy with Venetian blinds on the windows, halogen spots on the ceiling and fresh flowers on the bar. The back room has bare brick walls, subdued lighting and modern art.

At one end of the bar the kitchen servery puts out serious food by the table load (daily 12.00–15.00 & 18.00–22.00). Platters and *tapas* are one possibility or you can go for mains that range from sausages to sea bass cooked in a cosmopolitan range of styles, to be followed by sticky toffee pudding.

The highlights of a shortish beer list are Timothy Taylor's Landlord and Everards Tiger, each hand-drawn through glass cylinders on the bar, a method rarely seen nowadays but intended to instil confidence that the beer is well-kept.

Tiger Best Bitter is a much improved classical best bitter that is 'dry-hopped' to improve the initial flowery impact, which gives way to a long dry finish.

2–4 Moxon Street W1U 4EW

T 020 7935 0341

www.lafromagerie.co.uk

Baker Street

Sat 09.00–18.00; Sun 10.00–18.00; Mon 10.30–19.30
others 08.00–19.30

Frometon (7.0%)

Brasserie Artisanale des Deux Caps, Tardinghen, France

So now a cheese shop. Though not an ordinary cheese shop, if there is such a thing any more. Rather, a shop in which the selling of cheese is both a central and an inessential part of a delightful business.

The whole is housed in a pretty building – cheese to the right, the rest down an open passageway to the left, past baskets of fresh fruit and vegetables. Further on tables are spread with produce of all kinds arranged like snow, in drifts. Chocolates, bonbons, truffles, biscuits, sweets, sugared rose petals and nuts – no supermarket neatness in sight – and on to breads, pasta, honey and eggs.

The same display technique is accorded to the cheeses, the dried sausage and the charcuterie – they sell that too. No plastic wrapping. Proper food, properly presented. A dangerous place to shop when hungry.

To the rear of this scented hall is a small raised area for sampling. A large refectory-style table down its middle and a few small ones to the side. Snug.

This is an ideal place to try a plate of divine tasting cheese with a beer.

The owners recommend that the hand-made camembert from farmer Durand in Normandy is especially fine when paired with Frometon, a beer developed by brewer Christophe Noyon at his 2 Caps brewery, near Boulogne, in collaboration with cheesemonger Philippe Olivier.

Frometon is an amber coloured, strong beer in the Belgian triple style and its full, fruity, hoppy character compliments such a cheese better than any wine.

Golden Eagle

59 Marylebone Lane W1U 2NY

T 020 7935 3228

Baker Street & Bond Street

Sun 12.00–19.00

others 11.00–23.00

St. Austell Tribute (4.2%)

St. Austell Brewery Co., St. Austell, Cornwall

This is an old fashioned, basic bar with no frills, but has a good atmosphere when things get lively. On Tuesday, Thursday and Friday evenings from 20.30 they even wheel out the old upright near the front door for a sing-along round the old Joanna. *(Tourists please note: Cockney slang rhymes 'Joanna' with 'piano', while a 'sing-along' is exactly what it says.)*

The rest of the time this is just a small, friendly traditional pub lodged at the foot of a fine, Victorian four-storey building on the corner of Marylebone Lane and Bulstrode Street, with partial stained glass windows in a pretty green.

Seating is limited to a few tables and chairs towards the back of the room and stools along the bar and narrow shelf that runs along the windows.

There is no food but the management is happy for customers to bring their own sandwiches into the bar.

In the best tradition of an old-fashioned street corner pub the quality of the draught beer is exceptionally fine. Partly this is down to good cellar management and partly to choosing fine beers.

Cornwall's independent family brewery, St. Austell has been gaining a lot of prizes in the last few years under the stewardship of its Brewing Director Roger Ryman, formerly of Young's. As a consequence its beers are increasingly finding their way to London.

Tribute is now their biggest seller. Brewed using its own specially commissioned malt, Cornish Gold, this light amber best bitter greets you with an aroma of tangy, zesty American Willamette hops and follows through with a biscuity malt taste and long bitter finish.

35 Golden Lion

25 King Street SW1Y 6QY

T 020 7930 7227

Piccadilly Circus

CLOSED SUNDAY; Sat 11.00–19.00
others 12.00–21.00

Hogs Back TEA (4.2%)

Hogs Back Brewery, Tongham, Surrey

This attractive, bow-fronted pub near Christie's Auction House, is haunted by theatrical ghosts. Next door was once Queen Victoria's favourite St. James's Theatre, which in 1892 premiered Oscar Wilde's first play, Lady Windermere's Fan.

From 1950 it was managed by Laurence Olivier and his wife Vivien Leigh and although it closed in 1957, there remains a Theatre Bar upstairs, containing much memorabilia from and about those glorious days.

The pub's frontage is made up of wavy stained glass windows with panels displaying motifs of gold-maned lions, fruits, flowers and the face masks used in Greek drama. The front door leads into a wood-floored room with tall tables and stools, dominated by dark wood and a red ceiling.

They have met the challenge of the smoking ban by making over a tiny bowed balcony on the first floor, which holds four people at a time and overhangs the street, as an outside space for smokers – allowing them to take a fume with a view.

This is not a dining pub but food is served (Mon–Fri 12.00–21.00; Sat 12.00–16.00)

There is always a good selection of traditional draught beers including as a permanent fixture a beer called TEA, or Traditional English Ale, from the Hogs Back brewery in Surrey. The beer arrived, like the brewery, in 1992 and is now their flagship brand.

TEA is a classic best bitter, amber in colour and with a good balance of bitterness, malt and fruit character.

Green Man

36 Riding House Street W1W 7ES
T 020 7580 9087
➔ Oxford Circus & Goodge Street
Sun 12.00–22.30
others 12.00–23.00
Sierra Nevada Pale Ale (5.2%)
Sierra Nevada Brewing Co., Chico (California), USA

The external clue to the specialty of this pretty corner pub near Goodge Street tube station is found on its bright green sunshade. The apple logo marks it out as London's top cider bar.

Its pleasant main bar takes up the ground floor of a four-storey Victorian building, with wood flooring and comfortable banquette seating in British racing green to the rear. The back wall carries a striking painting of the pub itself in full swing.

A nice old wooden partition partly divides the front and rear portions of the bar. Note the original ceiling too, the old fireplace and some fine etched glass.

'Room 2' upstairs has a big screen that shows movies and sports channels.

The food is interesting, with home-made sausage rolls, corn-fed chicken burgers and a Caesar salad with anchovies & grilled chicken.

The matchless selection of ciders can stretch to ten on draught, including one produced for the pub, plus another five in bottles. Perversely perhaps, we are here for the beer, which comes from the Sierra Nevada Brewing Company in California.

A slightly stronger bottled version of Sierra Nevada Pale Ale can be found in many UK supermarkets nowadays but here the beer is on draught. It is a deep golden, fragrant, spritzy beer which flaunts its hops but is highly drinkable.

47 Chandos Place WC2N 4HS

☎ 020 7836 0291

www.harpbarcoventgarden.com

⊖ Charing Cross & Leicester Square

🕐 Sun 12.00–22.30
others 11.00–23.00

▐▐ **Black Sheep Best Bitter** (3.8%)

⊞ Black Sheep Brewery, Masham, North Yorkshire

Just off Trafalgar Square and parallel with the Strand, this fine little pub serves a busy part of central London. Be prepared to bustle.

The space by the long bar is too narrow for seats so enjoy some perpendicular drinking while gazing at the collection of picture portraits from the days when celebrity involved having charisma, or at least talent. There are handsome mirrors too, incorporating a Celtic knot motif round their edges.

The Celtic link is in the impressive green and gold frontage too, dominated by stained glass windows with, we think, Welsh harps.

Things widen out a bit beyond and to the rear of the bar, where there is room for a few table and stools. This also affords access to the upper floor where an oddly pink room in the manner of a 1950s boudoir houses ornate mirrors and more portraits.

The pub follows a simple but successful rule of catering, which is that if you do not have room for a proper kitchen, specialise. Here it is the prize winning O'Hagan's sausages, served with crusty bread – ideal company for a pint of ale.

Despite its size, popularity allows the Harp sufficient turnover to keep three regular and as many guest draught beers well. Timothy Taylor's Landlord and Harvey's Sussex are usually there and so is Black Sheep Best Bitter, from the brewery of the same name created by Paul Theakston in the days after his family's brewery went walkabout.

The Best Bitter is a light golden session beer that retains its refreshing character and hoppy bite right down to the last gallon.

de Hems

11 Macclesfield Street W1D 5BW

T 020 7437 2494

→ Piccadilly Circus

🕐 Sun 12.00–22.30

others 12.00–24.00

🍺 **La Trappe Tripel** (8.0%)

Trappistenbierbrouwerij De Koningshoeven, Tilburg, Netherlands

In the heart of London's China Town is this little bit of the Netherlands, though nowadays its ambience owes more to Belgian brewers and German painters.

Originally the Macclesfield, it was bought in 1890 by a Dutch sea captain called De Hem, who turned it into an oyster & stout bar. Upstairs the 'Oyster Room' was the place where thrifty Captain De Hem took used oyster shells and used them to plaster the walls. Rumour has it that over 300,000 were used over the years.

During the Second World War, this was the unofficial meeting place of members of the Dutch Resistance and it wears its Dutch connections proudly. There is an orange football shirt above the bar, stone *jenever* bottles for decoration and, yes, tulips on the tables in season. The name was changed to De Hems in 1959.

Those familiar with the tradition of the *kroeg* or Dutch brown café will note that its bar is laced down the side of its single rectangular room. Table service is offered (though usually ignored). Cable TV shows Dutch sporting events.

Of arguably less historical importance, this was the venue that hosted the comedy club where in 1998 a young Julian Barrett and Noel Fielding first created the Mighty Boosh.

Food is a kind of Anglo-Dutch fusion including the Dutch-leaning *erwten* (pea) soup and more Anglicised steak & ale pie.

Our favourite beer here is perhaps the best in all the Netherlands. La Trappe Tripel is brewed at the only Trappist brewery outside of Belgium, and is a hefty, amber-coloured ale with a fruity, bitter sweet character.

39–45 Bermondsey Street SE1 3XF
T 020 7403 6655
www.thehidebar.com
⊖ London Bridge
🕐 CLOSED SUNDAY; Sat 17.00–02.00
  others 10.00–24.00
▥ **Meantime Pale Ale** (4.7%)
✠ Meantime Brewing Co Ltd, Greenwich, London

Tucked down a back street near the busy London Bridge tube and rail hub, the Hide is an attractive little place specialising in everything drinkable, on the ground floor of the international Wine & Spirit Education Trust. No, really.

Modernist décor includes light fittings on shower flexes extruding from recessed ceiling voids moulded out of concrete, a riveted wood-tiled floor resembling ivory and architectural flowers in vases.

Relax on black sofas or café chairs and watch bar tenders throw cocktail bottles about. They have a tiny back room for chilling with loud wallpaper for those who prefer to stay frantic.

The food menu (12.00–16.00 & 17.30–22.00) changes daily as all ingredients are fresh. Anything from a burger to three-course dining is a runner, with a cured meat platter & toasted *ciabatta* and Neal's Yard cheese platter always available.

The Hide runs tasting events each Tuesday night which last about an hour and can include beer tasting with cheese. For details and reservations see their website.

Although the drinks focus is on the seriously expensive wine list and the impressive list of long, short and fancy cocktails, beer finds its place too.

As well as some international specialities they have three taps that rotate draught beers from Meantime, whose London Stout (6.5%) is also worth a punt. Meantime Pale Ale is sort of mid-Atlantic, amber and hoppy but featuring English Goldings alongside its American cousins.

Hobgoblin

21 Balcombe Street NW1 6HE

T 020 7723 0352

Baker Street & Marylebone

Sun 12.00–22.30

others 12.00–23.00

Hobgoblin (4.5%)

Wychwood Brewery, Witney, Oxfordshire

For those of a certain age the name Balcombe Street is usually associated with the word 'siege'. This pub's fifteen minutes of fame came from being right opposite no. 22b, where in December 1975 four IRA gunmen escaping from police kept its two occupants hostage for nearly a week before surrendering.

Nestled between Regents Park and Marylebone station, the Hobgoblin is a traditional looking ground floor corner pub in a building the real pedigree of which is revealed by looking at the flats above.

Inside is a comfortable, cosy bar with décor that mixes terrorism memorabilia with candles, skulls, goblins, witches, demons and a mock stuffed raven.

There is a cellar bar for hire, also kitted out with gnarled furniture of the spooky variety.

To accommodate the smoking ban, they allow the nicotine dependent to borrow a communal golfing umbrella when it is raining, on trust.

Food (Mon–Sat 12.00–16.30 & 18.00–23.00) is totally Thai and also available for take-away. The chef goes round the tables regularly taking food orders direct to the kitchen.

Oxfordshire's Wychwood Brewery and its parent company, Refresh UK, was taken over early in 2008 by the Marston wing of Wolverhampton & Dudley Breweries. It had become the third largest supplier of premium ales to the UK supermarket trade including Prince Charles' own Duchy Original beers.

Their sole year-round draught beer is Hobgoblin, a big, ruddy beer with bags of sweet malt and fruit.

28 Ivanhoe Road SE5 8DH

T 020 7733 4797

www.hoopersbar.co.uk

⇌ East Dulwich

🕐 Sat 14.00–23.00; Sun 15.00–23.00
others 17.30–23.00

🍾 **Black Boss Porter** (8.5%)

▭ Boss Browar Witnica SA, Witnica, Poland

Hoopers is a London community tavern of the future, with an emphasis on relaxation and great beers.

Formerly the Ivanhoe, it is a classically designed, wedge-shaped Victorian pub in an equally typical residential estate of the time. From its huge front facing picture windows you get a fine view down the hill you have probably just have climbed from the station.

The massive, half-wooden front room is divided by décor rather than partitions, though here is a cosy, wood-panelled snug out the back. A long curving bar runs throughout.

You can perch and watch the screen showing major sporting events or view the display cabinet of old brewing memorabilia that includes twin discouragements to beer drinking – a temperance movement pamphlet on the evils of drink and an illuminated Watney's Red Barrel sign. There are board games too.

Food is limited to *panini* and toasties.

On the tables are useful beer menus, describing the beer, its style and country of origin. There is a new European beer every month. British cask beers rotate and Belgian and German beers dominate the list of bottles. However, some useful Polish beers have also arrived – and not blond lagers either.

Although it was Czechoslovakia's brewers who reigned over the brewing world of the old Eastern bloc, strong black beers from Poland also survived the homogenisation of the Soviet era. Uncompromising Black Boss Porter, from western Poland, is just such a Baltic Porter with rich dark tones, slightly smoky, with a coffee taste.

Horseshoe

28 Heath Street NW3 6TE

T 020 7431 7206

→ Hampstead

🕐 Mon–Sat 10.00–23.00; Sun 10.00–22.30

🍺 **McLaughlin's Hampstead Summer** (3.6%)

🍻 McLaughlin's Brewery, Hampstead, London

When the accountants at JD Wetherspoon plc decided that the Three Horseshoes in Hampstead no longer fitted their corporate plan it was a great day for local beer drinkers. By May 2006, the newly single Horseshoe had re-opened with a total redesign, an Australian owner and its own microbrewery.

Just off Hampstead High Street, this self-styled 'brewhouse & dining pub' is now an open plan bar with white-painted bare brickwork, wood floors, long tables and odd wooden chairs. The light wood bar is adorned with huge lampshades and fresh flowers, with drinks dispense to the left and food to the right

The Horseshoe majors on good, gastro-pub fayre (Mon–Sat 12.30–15.30 & 16.30–22.00, Sun 12.00–16.30pm & 18.30–21.30) for as many generations of the Hampstead set as can elbow their way in.

For beer drinkers the draws are a plethora of good bottled beers from US micros, Belgium and Australia, a barrel of something from Adnams perched on the back of the bar and the home-brewed ale.

McLaughlin's beers are named after a North Queensland brewery in the family of owner Jasper Cuppaidge. Hampstead Summer is a golden ale that is available all year round. It has a fragrant hop and good citric body, with lots of peach and grapefruit character

Island Queen

87 Noel Road N1 8HD

T 020 7704 7631

⊖ Angel

◷ Thu–Sat 12.00–24.00
other days 12.00–23.00

▥ **Küppers Kölsch** (4.8%)

▬ Küppers Kölsch Brauerei, Köln (Cologne), Germany

The community pub, Islington style, which means quiz nights, comedy nights and other social events.

You will find it in a quiet spot, opposite a primary school, in a leafy residential part of the borough. The deep purple ivy clad exterior fronts a nicely designed old building with a reasonable number of old features such as curved glass front windows, a high patterned ceiling, dark brown woodwork and etched glass. The only bit that jars is the collection of odd ceiling lights, like a congregation of test tubes with bad nerves.

The central island bar curves round the light, squarish main public room. Another is a dark lounge-like place with low angular sofas. The last gains a conservatory feel from its faintly ridiculous giant mirrors adorned with textured palm trees and fronds.

There is a pleasant outside drinking area here when the weather is fine.

Food (12.00–22.00 with an afternoon gap on weekdays) is free range British, from posher sandwiches to thoughtfully raised steak & chips via broad bean, leek & pea risotto.

As well as the real ales and ciders on draught you can find Küppers Kolsch, one of the many 4.8% straw-coloured, top-fermented beers made to that style in the city of Köln (Cologne), its designation now protected by the EU. Deceptively light, sweetish and delicately hopped, it is often mistaken for a lager.

55 Britton Street EC1M 5UQ

T 020 7490 4281

www.stpetersbrewery.co.uk/london

Ǝ Farringdon

Ⓣ CLOSED SATURDAY & SUNDAY

others 11.00–23.00

▐▌▌ St Peter's Best Bitter (3.7%)

✚ St Peter's Brewery Co Ltd, St. Peter's South Elmham, Suffolk

There has been a Jerusalem Tavern in Clerkenwell since the 12th century and the current building dates from 1720, but this pub actually dates from 1996, when St Peter's Brewery renovated the former merchant's house and watchmaker's shop and got it licensed.

Inside are several tiny, low-ceilinged rooms, mostly on the ground floor. Wooden floors and settles, some blue and white Delft tile panels near the front door and a stuffed fox in a glass case at the rear gives an impression of timelessness.

Subdued lighting adds to an atmosphere unmarred by artificial noise. The single bar counter gets crowded as it doubles as a passageway to the room at the rear.

With limited space indoors and only a few tables and chairs outside, pavement drinking in the perpendicular is very much the norm here. Note the plated head of St John the Baptist on the pub sign.

Food includes baguettes, bangers and roasts but requires you to find a table.

This is the brewery's only London pub and it serves all of their many beers including the award winning Grapefruit Beer and the gluten-free beer. Six draught beers include the regular and the seasonal, plus the full range of distinguished and distinctively bottled ales.

St Peter's Best Bitter is a typically English bitter, with a nice balance of hops and malt, making a tasty but easy-drinking brew.

Kensington Arms

41 Abingdon Road w8 6AH
T 020 7938 3841
www.kensingtonarms.com
High Street Kensington
Sun 12.00–22.30
others 11.00–23.00
Doom Bar (4.0%)
Sharp's Brewery Ltd., Rock, Cornwall

Just off busy Kensington High Street, the traditional Victorian brick fascia of this thoroughly modern pub gives little away of its surprisingly successful, 21st century makeover.

Creating large, light open spaces in old pub buildings rarely works well but here it does, thanks in large part to the clever introduction of light into the room via deep skylights, illuminating by day pleasant light wooden floors, tables and low taupe chairs and high stools. The myriad of bare wood mirrors help too.

By night generous quantities of halogens in the sunken ceiling take over. The numerous large plasma screen TVs for sporting events are less intrusive than they sound, being sunk into the fitments above the bar and swivelled away from view when not in use.

There are old London Underground and Tram posters, photographs of footballers and along one wall an arresting giant triptych of its sister pub, the Mariners Rock, at Rock in Cornwall, home to Sharp's brewery.

Food (12.00–17.00) has a Cornish connection too, with much fish and designer pasties.

The house beer is Doom Bar, brewed at Rock. Beers from this dynamic Cornish micro are found increasingly across the capital. This, their flagship beer, is named after the sandbank at the mouth of the Camel estuary, a notorious danger to shipping.

The only dangerous thing about this flowery, fruity bitter is its superb drinkability.

Kris Wines

394 York Way N7 9LW

T 020 7607 4871

Caledonian Road & Kentish Town

Mon–Sat 13.00–23.00;
Sun 13.00–22.00

Felstar Original Shalford (4.0%)

Felstar Brewery, Felsted, Essex

Despite its name, this unassuming shop in a parade just off Camden Road, between Camden Town and Holloway has probably the best selection of quality beers north of the river and one of the best in the country.

Unlike your average off-licence this place has knowledge, mainly provided by its extraordinarily well-informed and enthusiastic owner, Krishna. In addition to the selection of wines and 150 British bottle-conditioned ales, he stocks over 250 Belgian beers, 80 German and 30 French.

Considering its size, London has pitifully few places serving the growing demand for quality beers to drink at home.

As well as having one of the widest selections, the prices here are also keen for the capital.

Among the British selection are a number from the Felstar Brewery, in rural mid-Essex, where Franco the brewer, when not pressing wine or cider, feeding his quails, pruning his vines, fattening his pigs, tending his geese, stroking his ferrets or coaxing his owl, brews some mean beers – about a dozen at the last count.

Original Shalford is his best seller, a bottle-conditioned, traditional bitter brewed from finest Maris Otter malted barley and three different hops.

92 Lamb's Conduit Street WC1N 3LZ
T 020 7405 0713
Russell Square
Sun 12.00–22.30
others 11.00–24.00
Young's Special London Ale (6.4%)
Wells & Young's Brewing, Bedford, Bedfordshire

Near to the site of Thomas Coram's Foundling Hospital for the 'exposed and deserted young children' of Georgian London and the internationally renowned Great Ormond Street Hospital for sick children, this lovely old pub has traditional design etched into its soul.

The green-tiled façade boasts a cute lambsy pub sign. Inside the centrepiece is a classic oval island bar, with snob screens down its sides. These window panels of frosted glass in mahogany frames at face height were capable of being swivelled shut so that customers could maintain some privacy.

Cut into the oval bar on the rear right hand side is a tiny snug, or 'donkey box', accommodating about three people. There is a polyphon near to the door – a huge mahogany music box that can still play 'Blue Danube' by arrangement in exchange for a charitable donation.

It is not all as old as the deep red and dark green colour scheme makes it appear. The tables supported by three iron legs with mythical ladies and leonine feet, are classic 1960s, albeit *en route* no doubt to the pub décor halls of fame.

The old black and white photographs on the walls include Max Beerbohm and Mrs Patrick Campbell – the sunken area at the back being now renamed the Empire Theatre bar.

Food (12.00–21.00) includes 1729 Celebration pie, fish & chips and smoked salmon with soda bread.

Although at least two quality Young's beers are available on handpull, we recommend a beer from the shelves. Special London Ale is a prize winning, bottle-conditioned, deep golden, strong ale, beautifully aromatic, with a rich malt flavour and full hop presence.

Lord John Russell

91–93 Marchmont Street WC1N 1AL
T 020 7388 0500
➤ Russell Square
Sat 12.00–23.00; Sun 12.00–22.30
others 11.00–23.00
Budvar Dark (4.7%)
Budějovický Budvar, České Budějovice, Czech Republic

Lord John Russell (1792–1878) was the son of the 6th Duke of Bedford. He was an MP for nearly half a century, in the last twenty of which he represented the City of London. He was the last Whig Prime Minister, his party morphing into the Liberals during his first term (1846–52). He was remarkably small, as is this pub.

Russell's family owned large parts of Bloomsbury, which is where this no-nonsense local is found, in a Victorian building in a mixed shopping area. Its small, irregularly shaped, single room bar has huge picture windows that are ideal for people-watching in the busy street outside.

It also has a nice outside drinking terrace to the side.

The interior is all pale blues and greens with columns having replaced dividing walls. The candles and fresh flowers on the tables seem right for one of the areas of central London that has regained some of its village-like atmosphere.

Lunchtime food (Mon–Sat 12.00–14.30) extends on Sundays (13.00–17.00) to include braised steak and good value roasts of beef, pork, lamb, chicken and gammon, with all the trimmings.

The Budweiser Budvar brewery in the Czech Republic is rightly famed for its blond lager. This was the first pub in Britain to stocks its *tmavé*, or dark lager, on draught, an equally enticing brew.

Budvar Dark is an easy drinking beer with a bitter chocolate aroma, biscuit malt body and a good roasted finish.

18–20 Creechurch Lane EC3A 5AY
T 020 7623 8813
www.lowlander.com

⊖ Aldgate

🕐 CLOSED SATURDAY & SUNDAY
others 11.30–23.00

🍾 **Christoffel Blond** (6.0%)

☰ Bierbrouwerij St. Christoffel,
Roermond, Netherlands

A little bit of Benelux in the shadow of the Gherkin.

The Lowlander and its sister pub in Drury Lane aim to 'bring the best of Dutch and Belgian café culture to London'. Belgium provides most of the food and drink, while the Netherlands brings the Grand Café concept.

This large, handsome place lodges in an impressive building with a glass frontage that seems to go on forever, deep in the City of London. Its long, long, long bar serves a huge space filled with pale wood and lit by halogen spots, its vanilla walls adorned with Belgian breweriana.

Continental-style table service operates throughout.

The selection of Belgian and Dutch beers tops 100 in bottle with a further 16 on tap. They will serve a selection of the latter in third of a pint glasses on a 'stick' of three or six beers if you like. Alternatively, go to one of their regular Beer Schools.

Food (all day) is pan-European and big, with Belgian leanings in the form of mussels, sausage with *stoemp*, and waffles.

Despite the heavy Belgian presence, one of the best beers on the list is from the St. Christoffel brewery, near the German border in Dutch Limburg. First brewed in 1986 it fast became the blond beer of choice among Dutch beer nuts.

Christoffel Blond is a clean tasting blond lager with the taste of fresh hops and a lingering floral finish. It comes in a flip top bottle and is unfiltered, leaving a light yeast sediment that you can leave in the bottle or include, as you wish.

Marquess Tavern

32 Canonbury Street N1 2TB

T 020 7354 2975

www.marquesstavern.co.uk

➔ Highbury & Islington

🕒 Fri 17.00–24.00; Sat 12.00–24.00; Sun 12.00–23.00

others 17.00–23.00

Ebulum Elderberry Black Ale (6.5%)

✕ Williams Brothers Brewing Co., Alloa, Scotland

Fine columns and capitals decorate the outside of this glorious Victorian edifice in leafy residential Canonbury, not far from Hugh Myddleton's aqueduct, built in 1613 to bring fresh water from Hertfordshire to the city of London.

Sadly the architectural merits stop at the front door, though the current owners have done a good job of salvaging the 'improvements' made by previous landlords to create an elegant dining area, an island bar with a wooden floor and furnishings and, well OK, Chesterfield sofas.

Award-winning food (18.00–21.30 daily, plus Sat 12.00–16.00, Sun 12.00–17.00) is traditional British with flair, imagination and a side order of great cooking. Owner Will Beckett wrote "An Appetite for Ale", the best British guide yet to matching food with beer.

Try pig's head terrine & pickled pear (with Young's Ram Rod), scallops & samphire (Kasteel Cru), courgette & cheddar crumble (Fraoch Heather Ale) or venison with red cabbage & red wine sauce (Brooklyn Lager). Oh try the bloody lot, why not!

On a list of over 40 beers the most eccentric are from William Brothers Brewing, specialists in recreating antique Scottish ales from traditional ingredients, including one said to have druidic origins and to be good for sciatica.

Ebulum Elderberry Black is mashed with roasted oats and has herbs added to the hop boil before being fermented with elder-berries to give a fruit aroma, roasted flavour and gentle finish.

Microbar

14 Lavender Hill SW11 5RW
T 0207 228 5300
www.microbar.org
⊖ Clapham Common
🕐 Mon–Fri 18.00–24.00;
   Sat & Sun 13.00–24.00
🍾 **Goose Island IPA** (5.9%)
▦ Goose Island Beer Co., Chicago, USA

The business card says, 'Big Beers in a small bar' and we would not argue with that. The forte of this particular Lavender Hill mob is to gather together beers from the world's great microbreweries, deliberately sidelining better known big name beer brands to the general good of humanity.

This place feels like a bar rather than a pub, though it has a nice garden in fine weather. The frontage is glass with a minimalist interior. There is no food to distract from the purpose of the place and the atmosphere is relaxed and friendly.

There is no beer menu. Above the bar a large blackboard lists some of the excellent selection, though this is a guide rather than a statement. The easiest thing to do is look in the fridges or ask the knowledgeable bar staff what's on.

At any one time they have over a hundred bottled beers from Belgium, the Netherlands, Germany, the Czech Republic, Britain, the US, Australia and Mexico, plus frequently changing draught beers from around the world.

The US is particularly well-represented, with beers from Liberty, Goose Island, Flying Dog, Great Divide and Left Hand usually available.

American microbrewers have a passion for imitating old beer styles with greater authenticity than the surviving examples.

Goose Island IPA was an early revival of a crisp and hoppy take on the old British style of export pale ale, and one of the range that made this one of America's most successful micros

Museum Tavern

49 Great Russell Street WC1B 3BA

T 020 7242 8987

Tottenham Court Road & Holborn

Sun 12.00–22.30

others 11.00–23.00

Theakstons Old Peculier (5.6%)

T & R Theakston, Masham, North Yorkshire

Opposite the gates of the British Museum, in the heart of Bloomsbury. Though nowadays it is a pretty conventional place there has been a pub here since the days when the area was hunting grounds.

Its single room has arched windows to the front, some with etched panels. Decorations have some original features such as a wooden-bossed divided ceiling, attractive coving, a wooden bar back with carved fluted columns, mirrors aplenty and even a few stained glass panels.

Food (11.00–22.00) is standard pub grub such as scampi, gammon & eggs and a pie of the day and can be eaten anywhere, including the pavement tables in summer.

The beer selection is mainly guest ales, with a teaser list on the blackboard of those that are 'coming soon'. Our featured beer is a permanent fixture.

Theakstons Old Peculier is synonymous with the real ale revolution of thirty years ago. The family brewery in North Yorkshire was sold off in the 1980s, but in 2003 was taken back under family ownership and is now run by the four Theakston brothers.

Note the correct spelling, which refers to an Official of the Peculier in Masham, a powerful role created by the Archbishop of York during the reign of William the Conqueror to keep the locals in line. Sadly its frequent misspelling accounts in large part for the plethora of patronisingly stupid beer names in real ale land.

It is a full-bodied, rich, dark ruby brown ale that should be drunk with respect.

Ely Court (off Hatton Garden) **EC1N 6SJ**

T 020 7405 4751

⊖ Chancery Lane & Farringdon

🕐 **CLOSED SATURDAY & SUNDAY**
others 11.00–23.00

▥ **Deuchars IPA** (3.8%)

✕ Caledonian Brewery, Edinburgh, Scotland

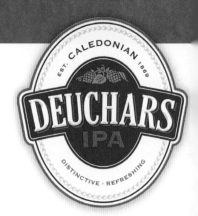

If you approach from Hatton Garden and keep your eyes peeled for a bishop's mitre in turquoise, you might just find Ye Olde Mitre Tavern in an alleyway between nos. 8 and 9, which leads to Ely Place.

The sign trumpets the fact that the original tavern was built in 1546, when it was within the grounds of Ely Palace, the London seat of power of the Bishop of Ely, which survived until its demolition, along with the original pub, in 1772. The pub was rebuilt later the same year.

Inside is a dimly lit and cosy series of three small rooms adorned with historic images, plus an upstairs saloon with a darts board – rare for central London. This place is famed for its great service and friendly staff.

An antediluvian cherry tree in a corner of the smaller front room is said to be an important ancient boundary marker for something or other. Outside is all woodwork and leaded lights, with enough room in the alleyway to drink outside when this little gem is full.

Food is limited to their famous toasties, scotch eggs and sausages. There is no extraneous noise-making machinery. Hoorah.

The excellent guest beer policy sees unusual cask beers drawn through its four handpulls. The constant presence is Deuchars IPA from whoever owns the Caledonian brewery nowadays.

This refreshing light session beer with a lingering floral bitterness is a favourite of Edinburgh's Inspector Rebus and his inventor, crime novelist Ian Rankin.

Oxo Tower Brasserie

Barge House Street SE1 9PH
T 020 7803 3888
〉 Blackfriars, Waterloo & Southwark
○ Sun 12.00–22.30
others 12.00–23.00
Meantime IPA (7.5%)
⊟ Meantime Brewing Co Ltd, Greenwich, London

The Oxo Tower has dominated the South Bank of the Thames, just down river from Blackfriars Bridge, since the original building received an Art Deco makeover in 1928. Seventy years later it won London's top award for urban regeneration, when it re-opened with an exhibition hall, shops and this top floor brasserie and restaurant.

Most people come here to enjoy cleverly constructed dishes from a modern menu, served by one of the best teams in London. The panoramic view north across the Thames from this eighth story vantage point is pretty stunning too, from both the glass-walled dining room and outside terrace.

Between lunch (12.00–15.00) and dinner (17.30–22.00) they serve a light menu, though the house marks of superb seafood, fusions of oriental and European cuisines and the creative use of market-fresh ingredients are still there.

One of a string of top quality restaurants around the kingdom to be owned by Harvey Nicks, the stylishly modern décor comes as little surprise. The similarly stylish, short but cleverly chosen list of beers might.

A dozen fine choices come from all over the world but we have chosen one from two miles down the river at Greenwich, where Meantime Brewing creates beers in classic styles, including this classical India Pale Ale.

IPAs were invented to survive a long sea journey from Britain to the outposts of Empire. They were brewed to above average strength with a high hop content, then put into completely filled oak casks for the six weeks passage to India.

Meantime IPA comes in 75cl bottles complete with a heavy sediment, so share with friends in a single pouring, ensuring it does not cloud more than necessary.

Pembury Tavern

90 Amhurst Road E8 1JH
T 020 8986 8597
www.individualpubs.co.uk/pembury
⇌ Hackney Central & Hackney Downs
🕐 Daily 12.00–23.00 (later sometimes)
🍺 **Sparta** (4.3%)
⊞ Milton Brewery, Milton, Cambridgeshire

There is something appealing in the idea that a small Cambridgeshire brewery can own a thriving pub in Hackney, supply it with up to 16 ever-changing real ales from its own range, while at the same time giving the locals a lesson in eco-friendly pub food, European brewing, Roman history and classical mythology.

The fine stone fascia fronts an ancient and modern interior. For once, a pub's innards have been ripped out to good effect, to create a huge, open, U-shaped room around a long, long bar. Herds of mismatched furnishings roam the plain wooden floor space. There are bar billiards and pool too.

The plain cream walls are decorated with old black and whites of the pub, pump clips and enough award certificates for everyone to get the message that Milton Brewery brews good ales.

Food (Mon–Sat 12.00–15.00 & 18.00–21.00; Sun 12.00–21.00) is 'locally sourced and home cooked'. Good vegetarian (barrel-aged *feta* cheese & chive salad), vegan (puy lentil aubergine & courgette bake) and carnivore (venison & beer stew). Meaty Sunday roasts also have a vegan option. The pork scratchings are home made.

Although the giant blackboard lists impressive bottled offerings particularly from Belgium (Oerbier, Hercule, Karmeliet Tripel) and Germany (Andechs Doppelbock, Spezial Rauchbier, Köstritzer Schwarzbier), it would be rude not to feature one of the brewery's forty or so regular beers.

Sparta is the pub's best selling beer, a golden pale bitter with lots of citrus hop character and a crisp bitterness.

Pig's Ear

35 Old Church Street sw3 5bs
T 020 7352 2908
www.turningearth.co.uk/thepigsear/thepigsear.htm
➤ South Kensington
☽ Mon–Sat 12.00–23.00; Sun 12.00–22.30
▌ **Pig's Ear Strong Beer** (5.0%)
☐ Uley Brewery Ltd., Uley, Gloucestershire

Just off Chelsea's famous King's Road, not far from Battersea Bridge and Chelsea Embankment, in an area famed for posh shopping is this exceptionally fine street corner pub that does everything well.

Its true island bar is wood-panelled and metal-topped, with an attractively mirrored backdrop that is echoed throughout the pub. It is hung with those oversized lampshades found in fashionable bars the world over – green (good) and fringed (not). The floors are in wood and ceiling in shiny red.

The design could come straight from the more moneyed parts of the Cornish Riviera, right down to the bijou, cabin-cruiser sized toilets. A semi-curtained-off side room is a tad nautical too, with pale blue-green panelling, odd melamine-type tables and stuffed fish.

Food (12.00–15.30, Sun 16.30 & 19.00– 22.30 Mon–Sat) trumps drinking with table reservations possible. The menu majors on shellfish and heavy red meat including game, with interesting veggie options. Roast bone marrow, hare & *foie gras* terrine, crab thermidore and butternut squash & broccoli ravioli.

Unsurprisingly perhaps the house beer is Pig's Ear from the excellent Uley Brewery, near Stroud in Gloucestershire, whose beers are brewed from Maris Otter malt with Hereford hops, making them high on flavour. The strongest in their range, it is both fruity and hoppy with a pleasantly bitter afterburn.

Porterhouse

21–22 Maiden Lane WC2 E7NA

T 0207 379 7917

www.porterhousebrewco.com /coventgarden.html

⊖ Charing Cross & Covent Garden

🕐 Fri & Sat 12.00–03.00; Sun 12.00–24.00
others 12.00–01.00

🍺 **Wrasslers 4X Stout** (5.0%)

🇮🇪 Porterhouse Brewing Co., Dublin, Ireland

The state of Irish brewing is a national disgrace, with perhaps the single exception of Dublin's Porterhouse Brewing Company. This pub is their Central London presence, built on the site of the birthplace of William Turner (1775–1851), who painted 'The Fighting Temeraire', Britain's best-loved picture.

The painting depicts an old man o' war sailing ship being towed to her last berth by an iron-clad steamer that symbolises a new era. Turner refused to sell it in his lifetime. It works at many levels, but not as many as the Porterhouse, which we are told has thirteen.

Forget the tacky Irish pub concept, this is a spacious tribute to real hospitality and the magnificence of beer culture. We cannot hope to describe its many floors, mezzanines and bar rooms. There are a lot – OK?

High ceilings, stone floors, generous wood fittings, tiled walls, copper piping everywhere, iron work, big rivets and a giant mechanical clock. It can only be heard at rare times when the pub is not heaving.

Food ranges from rock oysters and Irish stew to *meze* and *nachos* via Sunday roasts. Wednesday to Saturday has live music with traditional Irish on Sunday afternoons. They have a stout festival around St. Patrick's Day.

The choice of draught and bottled beers is so vast that they have a booklet. Bottles come mainly from Belgium, Germany, France and others. However, the house beers are brewed in Ireland and get shipped across with the cheeky but accurate claim that they come from "the world's largest genuine Irish Brewery".

Instead of Ireland's most famous stout or the two also-rans, they have their own excellent Plain Porter, Oyster Stout (yes – real oysters!) and our chosen beer Wrasslers 4X Stout. Drink these and understand what real Irish beer culture is about – and just how far it needs to go before it can climb back.

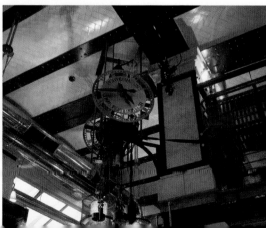

Portobello Gold

95–97 Portobello Road W11 2QB

T 020 7460 4912

www.portobellogold.com

Notting Hill Gate

Fri & Sat 10.00–00.30; Sun 12.00–23.30
others 10.00–24.00

Watou's Wit (5.0%)

Van Eecke, Watou, Belgium

Oh dear Notting Hill. Carnival. Portobello Market. Hugh Grant being nice.

Halfway down the hill that is Portobello Road, evergreen and all-purpose Portobello Gold is surrounded every Saturday by the world's largest portable junk shop and passed every August by the country's most famous and nerve-wracking street parade.

For the rest of the time this is a bar, restaurant, internet café, music venue and small hotel. Most of all it is a survivor.

The simple public bar is tiled, with bar stools round its curving bar and at its window. Saloon-style swinging doors lead to smarter areas at the rear, where the Oyster Bar eating area is populated with small snug areas divided by high-backed comfortable seats.

There is a 'tropical' conservatory restaurant with a suitably jungled theme and wicker seating. Walls are adorned with pictures of legendary musicians, reflecting the interesting mix of blue grass, jazz, rock and blues.

They have seven guest rooms above, one with roof terrace and putting green!

The beer list is a mix of InBev and good, with a couple of cask beers always available. The most interesting beer here, thus far unique in London, is the Belgian wheat beer, Watou's Wit.

Considered by some the best wheat beer in the world, Watou's Wit has all the usual characteristics of Belgian wheat beer – hazy, sweetish and spicy – but with a heavy hint of lemon and Curaçao.

Prague

5 Kingsland Road E2 8DA
T 020 7739 9110
www.barprague.com
Old Street
Sun 11.00–22.30
others 11.00–23.00
Bohemia Regent Dark (4.4%)
Bohemia Regent, Trebon, Czech Republic

The old East End always had a Bohemian streak. It is good to see it back even if it is a bit more literal.

Although the theme here is decidedly Czech, there are no austere, high-back seats or scrubtop tables. Rather, its small rectangular bar has white walls, exposed brick and some photo-montage-poster-splattered panels. The photographs on sale totter between art and soft-porn.

The wooden floor is sprinkled with a dozen or so café tables and oddly mismatched red Chesterfields at the rear. Very European. Indeed, you could be anywhere in Europe.

There are toasted bagels and snacks at the bar all day, plus pickles to go with them.

The drinks theme is decidedly Czech – they even stock Becherovka, the unquestionably 'acquired' tasting, clove-laden tonic that kept Czech national pride afloat during the Soviet era, from Karlovy Vary. Wusses can have a cocktail instead.

Draught beers include Budvar Blond and Dark, plus Pilsner Urquell. But it is the bottled beers that are unusual – possibly the best bottled Czech selection of any bar in London and including beers from Zatec, Krusovice and Lobkowicz.

There has been a brewery at Trebon since 1379. Its dark lager is a more modern invention and a sign of post Soviet liberation.

Pride of Spitalfields

3 Heneage Street E1 5LJ

T 020 7247 8933

⊖ Aldgate East

🕐 Fri & Sat 11.00–02.00
others 11.00–23.00

🍺 **Brewers Gold** (4.0%)

⊞ Crouch Vale Brewery, South Woodham Ferrers, Essex

The East End's Brick Lane has been synonymous with Indian restaurants for so long that few can remember the days when it was home of an East End scourge that threatened the very foundations of British culture. We refer to Watney's brewery and its terrible twins, Red Barrel and the Party Seven.

The small-paned windows and lace curtains of the Pride of Spitalfields, just off Brick Lane, looks like a neatly kept home but inside it is all pub. Its main bar and tiny, wood-clad snug are cosy, with button bench seating and stools, if you are lucky enough to find a seat.

There is a fire in cold weather and an outside drinking area in summer. Entertainment ranges from a pull-down TV screen for sporting events to a piano. There are black and whites of the old East End and interesting framed commercial documents on the walls, plus a collection of old bottles in the snug.

People really do come from miles around for the beer and its selection of guest beers is tempting. The Essex brewery Crouch Vale has the unique distinction of winning CAMRA's Champion Beer of Britain award two years running (2005 & 2006) with its Brewers Gold. It regularly appeared here even before its fame.

Brewers Gold is a quaffable pale golden ale with massive hop, grapefruit and citrus presence, which still manages to be light and refreshing.

Prince Alfred

5a Formosa Street W9 1EE

T 020 7286 3287

→ Warwick Avenue

🕐 Sun 12.00–22.30

others 12.00–23.00

🍺 **Young's Bitter** (3.7%)

🍻 Wells & Young's Brewing, Bedford, Bedfordshire

One of the finest examples of grand Victorian pub design in London – inside and out – is found where this residential street meets a street of shops in deepest Maida Vale.

Built in 1856 and refitted in 1898, its front fascia consists of beautifully waved glass in etched panels, held in place by delicate mahogany surrounds that snake in and out at fantastic angles. Glass reaches from waist to ceiling height, creating an airy interior.

Five classically inspired broken pediment mahogany partitions divide the pub into as many rooms, each with its own street entrance. The partitions are low enough to display the interior as a whole. Its only nod to modernity is high wood tables, stools and benches that are difficult to mount or dismount gracefully.

The central island bar, in mahogany and etched glass, is a confection of prodigious proportions towering above proceedings, adorned with wrought iron and topped with classical urns. Its clock – similar to that in the Princess Louise (next page) but more elegant – is stuck permanently at half past one.

Between rooms are tiny doorways, a metre high and narrow, through which braver customers occasionally squeeze themselves, like Alice entering Wonderland.

Try to ignore the architecture of the incongruous restaurant at the rear (daily 12.00–15.00 & 18.30–22.30).

What better place to drink Young's Bitter, an excellent session beer with a soft fruity flavour and satisfying bitter finish, recently moved from its base in Wandsworth to a new home in Bedford.

62 Princess Louise

208–209 High Holborn WC1V 7BW

T 020 7405 8816

⊖ Holborn

🕐 Sat 12.00–23.00; Sun 12.00–22.30
others 11.00–23.00

▥ **Samuel Smith Old Brewery Bitter** (4.0%)

▦ Samuel Smith Old Brewery, Yorkshire, UK

This fabulous Victorian pub is named after the brightest, most interesting and longest lived of Queen Victoria's six daughters. She married a nobleman so lowly that he was technically a commoner and became an MP. She championed university education for women and survived to see the outbreak of the Second World War.

The Princess Louise was built originally in 1872, though much of its current effects date from an 1891 refurbishment. It re-opened in January 2008 after a lengthy closure for renovation by its owners, Yorkshire brewers Sam Smiths.

Attractive enough from the outside, with its red granite pillars and decorative capitals, it is inside that is the absolute antithesis of modern, pared-down, minimalist décor. This is late Victorian pub design gone ape, with a riot of mosaic flooring, etched glass, glazed tiles, gilt mirrors and stained glass.

Slim Corinthian columns support a heavily plastered, patterned high ceiling. The refurbishment is a triumph of re-creation, with some parts returned to their original design, such as the floor-standing, mahogany framed, etched glass panels that divide the pub into five tiny front rooms and two larger back areas.

On entering the pub from either of its swing doors at the front, the effect is like entering a 'house of mirrors', with the incoming customer needing to make his way down the glazed side passages of the pub to select a room.

All seven areas access the horseshoe-shaped central bar with its magnificent mahogany four-faced tower clock, complete with pinnacles, resembling a mini version of Big Ben.

Far from the replaced screens obscuring the light, they make the place feel brighter than it was, assisted by a toning down of the deep red and gold ceiling and the return of dark wooden floors to a lighter hue.

Sit back with a beer and marvel at the forces that must have driven the late Victorians to create such grand designs, and be grateful for the skills of the latter day craftsmen, designers and brewery execs who enabled it to be returned to full pomp.

If gawping becomes boring, try finding how many different species of flower and plant you can locate carved into the glass and fired into the tiles, from roses to hops to, er, bulrushes.

The rear staircase leads up to a lower key lounge with sofas and fires and a small bar for ordering food. For half the population it also leads down to what is the pub's *pièce de resistance*, an original triple-stall, porcelain gentlemen's urinal.

The route descends into a *fin de siècle* nightmare, as the glazed tiling becomes more frenzied in quantity, texture and colour before the relief afforded by an opportunity to pass water over a veritable antique. Ladies must satisfy themselves with a more contemporary and functional facility.

Oh yes, and the beer. Sam Smith's only real ale is Old Brewery Bitter, a chestnut brown, Northern bitter built on malt, from the aroma right through to the aftertaste.

43 St. Johns Hill SW11 1TT

T 020 7585 1549

⇌ Clapham Junction

🕐 Fri & Sat 17.00–01.00; Thu 17.00–24.00
others 17.00–23.00

🍾 **Doggie Style Classic Pale Ale** (5.5%)

▬ Flying Dog Brewery, Denver, USA (Colorado)

Project Orange is a couple of minutes walk up the hill from Clapham Junction station but a world away from the clone bars that litter the local high streets. If you tend to the view that the cynical creators of those predictable chains are marginally less imaginative than the sheep who graze there, you might love this place.

Project Orange has chosen its own direction, which is indie rock paired with good beer. Its windows display its music policy and you regularly hear tunes from the likes of Fugazi, We Are Scientists, Kooks, Dirty Pretty Things, and Datsuns. They also regularly showcase local live bands and labels in the venue downstairs. The music policy is not aimed at everyone – which is the point, actually.

The local label policy applies to the beers available too. An exceptional selection of bottled beer includes Power Station Porter from Battersea Brewery up the road but also a lot of good American stuff.

The Flying Dog Brewery of Denver, Colorado commissions the Wild Goose brewery of Frederick in Maryland to make their Flying Dog Doggie Style Classic Pale Ale, a classic stateside hoppy amber ale from a company whose strapline matches the attitude of this bar, 'Good Beer, No Shit.'

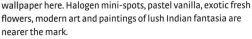
41 Buckingham Gate SW1E 6AF

T 020 7821 1899

www.thequilonrestaurant.com

St. James's Park & Victoria

Sat 18.00–23.00; Sun 12.00–15.30; 18.00–22.30

others 12.00–14.30; 18.00–23.00

Pietra (5.6%)

SA Brasserie Pietra, Furiani, Corsica, France

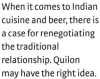

When it comes to Indian cuisine and beer, there is a case for renegotiating the traditional relationship. Quilon may have the right idea.

At the front of St James Court (now Buckingham Gate), this most superior of Indian restaurants, which describes its food as South Indian coastal with a contemporary twist, was one of the first in Britain to get a Michelin star.

No 20-watt light bulbs and red flock wallpaper here. Halogen mini-spots, pastel vanilla, exotic fresh flowers, modern art and paintings of lush Indian fantasia are nearer the mark.

The menu is a treasure to read. Why not a guinea fowl stew or roasted marinated tilapia fillet in plantain leaf? Copious fish and seafood dishes include popular crab cakes and a signature dish of baked black cod.

Chef Sriram Vishwanathan Aylur is especially interested in food and beer pairings and reflects this with a small but perfectly formed beer list matched to these styles of food.

OK, they do have Kingfisher but there are also lagers from Dutch brewer Lindeboom and the Brooklyn Brewery. Little Creatures from Western Australia and St Peter's from northern Suffolk appear too but the real find is the two beers from Corsican independent, Pietra.

Pietra itself is made in part from sweet chestnut flour, not simply as a flavouring but also providing some brewing sugar. The resulting reddish amber beer is sweet and spicy, well up to complimenting even the most assertive of dishes.

14 Winchester Walk SE1 9AG

T 020 7407 0557

London Bridge

CLOSED SUNDAY; Sat 10.00–23.00
others 12.00–23.00

Aecht Schlenkerla Rauchbier (5.1%)

Heller-Bräu Trum KG, Bamberg, Germany

This tiny bar, just round the corner from London's oldest fine foods emporium, Borough Market, is easily missed. At 13 feet by 7 it is London's smallest pub.

Its tiny drinking area has a white panelled ceiling. Most people remain standing though there are a couple of tall thin tables and stools. A slightly larger, decked outdoor drinking area is all but covered by an unfeasibly large umbrella with integral heaters – a non-smoking area when the umbrella is open.

Food is limited to baguettes, soup, pork pies and nibbles.

Size isn't everything though, at least not when it comes to keeping beer. For that they use Utobeer, the Borough Market beer stall. The list runs to over 130 and comes from most of the great beer drinking nations of the world, plus a few others. If in doubt, peek at the eye-level fridges or ask the knowledgeable staff.

Two handpulls draw ever-changing cask ales and six other fonts dispense German, Belgian and American beers.

Among the bottled beers regularly available is the remarkable Aecht Schlenkerla Rauchbier smoked brown lager, from the only brewing town in the world to have been made a UNESCO World Heritage site, the Franconian city of Bamberg.

Brewed with carefully wood-smoked malt before being lagered in natural cool cellars below Stephansburg hill, this fabulous beer has a smoky bacon aroma that can pervade the whole room. Your next beer will have no chance.

Roebuck

50 Great Dover Street SE1 4YG

T 020 7357 7324
www.theroebuck.net

⊖ Borough

🕐 Fri & Sat 12.00–01.00
others 12.00–24.00

🍺 **Pure Ubu** (4.5%)

➕ Purity Brewing Co., Great Alne, Warwickshire

Once upon a time, the Roebuck was London's 'first and last' London pub on the way to and from the port of Dover, the gateway to continental Europe. So much traffic stopped here that it needed four entrances.

It stands in a magnificent, much-gabled and chimneyed building at the junction of Trinity Street and Great Dover Street.

The original design and fittings are not much in evidence inside, though an airport lounge effect is avoided thanks to the enormous expanse of arched windows to the front, overlooking the drinking terrace and the huge oval bar in the centre from which spring some nice old supporting columns.

The walls are in brown and red, with striking art appended and a magnetic letter board for the more literary. Tables are scrub-topped in pale wood with similar effect chairs amid the ubiquitous Chesterfields.

An upstairs room hosts quizzes, big screen sports and, on alternate Thursdays, live music.

Big food (Mon–Fri 12.00–14.30 & 17.00–22.00, Sat&Sun 12.00–21.00) features a lot that is home-made, from *hummus* with pitta bread to special burgers and a steak & ale pie. Excellent breakfasts at the weekend and good Sunday roasts too.

On the beer front they feature Meantime's Viennese Amber lager, Helles blond lager and Wheat, er, wheat beer as well as two quality real ales from Purity Brewing in rural Warwickshire, Pure Gold and Pure Ubu.

Pure Ubu is a marvellously distinctive, full-flavoured amber ale named, we think, after the mascot dog who appears on the pump clip, and has nothing to do with Pere Ubu, the frequently self-regenerating underground rock band from Ohio.

128–132 Borough High Street SE1 1LB
T 020 7407 4057
www.roxybarandscreen.com
⊖ Borough
🕐 Fri & Sat 12.00–01.30 or later; Sun 12.00–24.00
others 17.00–24.00 or later
🍾 **Brooklyn Double Chocolate Stout** (10.1%)
🏳 Brooklyn Brewing Co, New York, USA

How to explain? The Roxy Bar and Screen is a kind of a cinema cum nite spot except that it is not at all tacky and most of the screenings are free and anyway it is the beer and the sit back and relax armchairs that will keep you coming back.

Ignore the unpromising modern fascia and front bar and head towards the back of the ground floor to find the giant bar and gigantic auditorium, its ceiling black, walls hung with red velvet drapes and huge screen showing anything from black & white clips of jazz films with the sound turned off, through to official screenings.

Some scheduled films rate a small cover charge but most of the time entrance is free provided you are drinking or dining. Seating is on a first come, first served basis. Ordering and service continue throughout.

A sort of over-sized pub cabaret effect is created by red lamps, Chesterfield sofas and armchairs and a myriad of mismatched wooden tables and chairs.

The food (most opening hours) is sold as *meze* except that it is really more *tapas*-meets-*taverna*, with all day roasts featuring every Sunday (from 13.00).

The impressive bottled beer list is sourced from the excellent Utobeer beer shop on Borough Market and has numerous highlights, from which we have chosen Brooklyn Double Chocolate Stout from Garret Oliver's wonderful Brooklyn Brewery, just off New York's East river, which has been making its entertaining beers since 1987.

Brooklyn Double Chocolate is a massive beer, brewed in the Imperial Russian Stout style. It pours solid, jet black with a thick mocha-like head, with an aroma of coffee and dark chocolate. Its initial sweetness gives way to a deep roasted malt and bitter chocolate coffee taste, and a surprisingly dry hoppy finish.

Royal Exchange

26 Sale Place W2 1PU

T 020 7723 3781

Paddington & Edgware Road

Sat 11.00–17.00; 19.00–23.00;
Sun 12.00–16.00; 19.00–22.30
others 11.00–23.00

Timothy Taylor's Golden Best (3.5%)

Timothy Taylor & Co, Keighley, West Yorkshire

This tiny tile-fronted corner pub is a real no-nonsense, old-fashioned place within an easy walk of Paddington Station. It has a strong Irish following though there is none of the chainstore Celtic or stick-on *craic*.

Its single bar makes clear it is a horse racing pub, with pictures, memorabilia and the TV screens to show the big races. There is a small drinking area at front. This is a great place to be during the Cheltenham Festival or on St. Patrick's day.

The distinctly carnivorous menu features roasts of Limerick ham, leg of pork, English lamb and rib of beef served with mash, seasonal vegetables and gravy. There are roast meat sandwiches too plus other snacks. Salt beef appears every Friday.

Perhaps surprisingly there are sixteen wines by the glass. The many empty jeroboam champagne bottles that decorate the place suggest that big wins should be shared.

The consistently excellent quality real ales always include bitters from Adnams and Brakspears but the top flight beer featured here is Timothy Taylor' Golden Best – another from the makers of Landlord. How do they pack so much flavour into such an innocent light mild? Small but perfectly formed.

44 Tabard Street SE1 4JU

T 020 7357 7173

⊖ Borough

🕐 Sat 12.00–23.00; Sun 12.00–18.00
others 11.00–23.00

▥ **Sussex Dark Mild** (3.0%)

✠ Harvey & Son, Lewes, East Sussex

In our view one of London's top pubs.

The only pub in London owned by and tied to the lovely Harvey's brewery of Lewes, near the Sussex coast, the Royal Oak was resurrected in 1997. It prides itself on being a traditional ale house, offering a genuinely warm welcome, top quality ales and good value food, eschewing all noise-making machines.

On the corner of a handsome building constructed in the 1870s, its exterior has traditional black and white paintwork and original tawny tiles still present.

Its two rooms have wooden floors, tables and chairs. Windows from waist height to ceiling afford the front bar natural light by day. Unusually, in order to get to the other room you need to cross behind the bar, causing all English drinkers to make vague, guilty, hurrying movements as they shuffle through.

There is a meeting room upstairs for hire.

Food (Mon–Sat 12.00–14.45; Sun 12.00–16.30) is traditional pub grub done well. There are doorstep sandwiches, pies and steak & chips. There is also a good selection of wines, plus ciders from Weston's of Much Marcle in Herefordshire.

All of Harvey's regular and seasonal real ales are served on handpull, including their Sussex Dark Mild. This classic southern take on English dark mild gets its colour, aromas and caramel finish from dark roasted malts. It is another great example of how British brewers manage to pack a lot of taste into a low strength brew.

Seven Stars

53 Carey Street **WC2A 2JB**
T 020 7242 8521
➔ Temple & Holborn
🕐 Sat 11.00–23.30; Sun 12.00–22.30
others 11.00–23.00
|||| **Adnams Broadside (4.7%)**
⊞ Adnams Brewery, Southwold, Suffolk

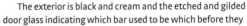

This ancient little pub, tucked just behind the Royal Courts of Justice, celebrated its 400th anniversary in 2002. It is a matter of judgement whether landlady Roxy Beaujolais is more or less famous than her cat, Thomas Paine. If not present in person, his mouse-munching skills are celebrated photographically on the wall.

The exterior is black and cream and the etched and gilded door glass indicating which bar used to be which before they were equalised. Built into and under the windows are glass-fronted faux cabinets of curiosities housing taxidermy, bones, skulls and coprolite, with commentaries.

The bar counter and narrow pub spreads out right and left, with a successful mix of old and new. Raspberry and plum coloured paintwork is set off against wood panelling, with small carpeted snugs off the main wooden-floored bar area.

Décor is black cats and barristers. Advocates' wigs lie in boxes near the window. Old film and advertising posters have the same themes. A perilous staircase leads to the toilets.

Guest beers are available but Adnams Bitter and Broadside are permanent fixtures. The latter is named after the 1672 naval battle of Sole Bay, against the Dutch, which was engaged just off the Suffolk coast near the brewery's home town of Southwold.

Broadside is a difficult-to-classify, deep copper coloured ale with an aroma of flowers, tangy fruit and biscuits, with a rich, spicy hop taste and a long, lingering, dry finish.

Ship & Shovell

1–3 Craven Passage WC2N 5PH

T 020 7839 1311

Charing Cross & Embankment

CLOSED SUNDAY

others 11.00–23.00

Badger First Gold (4.0%)

Hall & Woodhouse, Blandford Forum, Dorset

A pub of two halves – literally. Two bars on either side of an alley, linked by a common cellar and license.

Orientate yourself by the ceilings. The larger, smarter main bar has a mustard yellow one. The smaller gem of a bar has the reddest and shiniest ceiling you will ever see in a pub.

The smaller bar is a narrow wooden floored room with a couple of private alcoves opposite its tiny bar counter. Its walls have avoided mock surfaces, retaining a coat of grained paint on top of ancient, possibly original timber and plaster panels. The rear snug is very, with room for one tiny table and two chairs.

The pub is named after Sir Cloudesley Shovell, a 16th century seafaring man, whose biography is displayed to the right side of the bar, near a portrait of the man. Sir Cloudesley survived a shipwreck off the Isles of Scilly, only to be foully set upon and murdered by a woman on reaching the shore, for his emerald ring.

Above the smaller bar is the Crow's Nest, a charming upstairs bar reached via a wooden staircase that creaks like old ships timbers. It feels more like the Captain's cabin and, like the rest of the pub is adorned by pictures of ships.

Most parts of the pub can be hired for private parties.

The Ship & Shovell is tied to the Hall & Woodhouse brewery, whose three regular Badger beers appear in both bars, with a seasonal beer in the larger bar. Badger First Gold is a newish golden ale, typical of the style, with a slight grapefruit character.

67–77 Charterhouse Street EC1M 6HJ

T 020 7251 7950

www.smithsofsmithfield.co.uk

→ Farringdon & Barbican

Sat 10.00–23.30; Sun 09.30–22.30; Thu & Fri 07.00–23.30
others 07.00–23.00

Wooden Hand Brewery Cornish Buccaneer (4.3%)

Wooden Hand Brewery, Truro, Cornwall

This four-storey bar and restaurant is housed in a huge, long, arched warehouse building directly opposite Smithfield meat market.

The ground floor bar is a large, modern square with an unavoidable open aluminium kitchen taking up most of one side of a room drizzled with industrial strength ducting and naked concrete floors and seats for the lucky few.

A brightly lit theatrical lift with a red plush interior, leads not to a bordello but to the other dining rooms that get more expensive as you go up. The gentlemen's convenience extends as far as a bloke who squirts soap and runs water for you.

Music is lively and loud.

Although many of the beers to be found here are mainstream, there is an unusual offering from the Wooden Hand brewery of Truro, which derived its name from the startlingly lifelike prosthetic hand of Cornishman John Carew who lost the original while fighting Spaniards at the siege of Ostend (1601–04). Its articulated fingers were brass-jointed and it became a family heirloom.

Their Cornish Buccaneer is a bottled pale ale with a suitably piratical label featuring a skull in a tricorn hat with crossed cutlasses. It pours golden copper and has a dominant hop aroma and taste.

73 Spice of Life

6 Moor St W1D 5NA

T 020 7437 7013

www.spiceoflifesoho.com

Tottenham Court Road & Leicester Square

Sun 12.00–22.30
others 11.00–23.00

McMullen's Cask Ale (3.9%)

McMullen & Sons, Hertford, Hertfordshire

This fine late Victorian pub sits at the busy Cambridge Circus, nestled between the huge Cambridge pub on one side and the even larger Palace Theatre on the other. The 1890s was a busy decade for architects of public houses in London.

The Spice of Life does comfort the old-fashioned way, with wood panelled walls and classically-inspired gold acanthus-leaved wallpaper. The front bar has a startling tartan carpet with a plainer wooden raised floor nearer the bar. Stripy banquette seating and crystal chandeliers top off its elegance.

The kitchen (daily 12.00–21.00) offers pub staples like sausage & mash, burgers and sandwiches, plus more adventurous *tortilla*-crusted chicken with a black olive mash with a cherry tomato and thyme sauce. There are spiced doughnuts and waffles too.

The pub has played an active part in London's live music scene for some decades, the Backstage Bar downstairs now being a renowned jazz venue.

It is tied to McMullen's brewery of Hertford and stocks all its beers. Cask Ale is the newest addition to the range, a draught amber beer with a malty aroma and citrus hop flavours throughout. An excellent, light session beer.

6 Belgrave Mews West SW1X 8HT
T 020 7235 3019
→ Victoria & Hyde Park Corner
🕐 Sun 12.00–22.30; Sat 12.00–23.00
others 11.00–23.00
▮▮ **Chiswick Bitter** (3.5%)
⊟ Fuller Smith & Turner, Chiswick, London

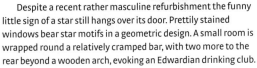

In mews not far off Belgrave Square, this incongruously simple pub for decades slaked the thirst of servants from the grand houses around. It is now the haunt of staff from the embassies and national institutions that litter Belgravia.

Despite a recent rather masculine refurbishment the funny little sign of a star still hangs over its door. Prettily stained windows bear star motifs in a geometric design. A small room is wrapped round a relatively cramped bar, with two more to the rear beyond a wooden arch, evoking an Edwardian drinking club.

Ornate gilt mirrors are interspersed with caricatures and silhouettes. Prints, paintings and drawings appear too. Each room has a fine fireplace that, famously and at great effort, still boasts a real fire.

The wooden floors are gingered up by rich central carpets in red, dark blue and gold, supporting a motley selection of padded benches, semi-upholstered dining chairs and dark bucket seats. Ceiling mouldings leap out in deep relief above walls painted in restrained buff, with occasional splashes of burgundy.

There is an absolute ban on street drinking here – doing so will get you thrown in.

Upstairs is an elegant book-lined dining room (Mon–Fri 12.00–16.00 & 17.00–21.00; Sat & Sun 12.00–17.00), with Vintage Dom Perignon at £150 a bottle making an odd accompaniment to upmarket liver & bacon or cod & chips.

The Star carries all of Fullers beers in perfect condition. It has been in all 36 editions of CAMRA's Good Beer Guide, including the Gestetner-printed prototype of 1973.

Chiswick Bitter is their lunchtime beer, a fresh, flowery, subtly hopped star.

St. Stephen's

10 Bridge Street SW1A 2JR

T 020 7925 2286

⊖ Westminster

🕐 Fri 10.00–24.00; Sat 10.00–23.30;
Sun 11.00–22.30
others 10.00–23.30

▒ Tanglefoot (4.9%)

⊞ Hall & Woodhouse, Blandford Forum, Dorset

Opposite the Houses of Parliament, this handsome Westminster pub has the feel of a long serving institution, though it had been closed for some while before its 2003 refurbishment by brewers Hall & Woodhouse.

The smallest of its three rooms is at the front, with a minstrel's gallery. A larger rear room has a separate bar. Upstairs is a comfortable area with armchairs and secluded alcoves. The oddly serpentine bar is a work of art in itself, snaking diagonally across the room.

The pub's design is suitably Puginesque, from the finely ornamented high ceilings, carved wood and etched glass to the opulent wallpaper. Green leatherette high-backed wall seating in the front bar alludes to the House of Commons, the divisional bell for which is relayed to the pub to call back stray MP's who may need to vote.

The potted palms do not obscure the wonderful view of St Stephen's Tower, which houses the bell called Big Ben. Another institution is displayed above the gentlemen's urinals – the letters page of the Daily Telegraph.

Food (daily to 22.00) includes an all day breakfast, fish & chips, bangers & mash, ham & eggs and the house speciality, 'Sussex Smokey' – white and smoked fish with spinach in a cheese sauce.

The best known beer from the so-called Badger brewery is Tanglefoot, a best bitter that the British think is strong. It is light amber in colour, full-bodied and hits all the right notes.

Tate Modern

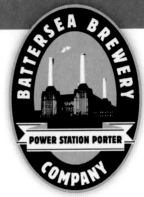

Bankside SE1 9TG
T 020 7887 8888
www.tate.org.uk/modern/eatanddrink/restaurant.htm
➔ Blackfriars & Southwark
🕐 Fri & Sat 10.00–21.30 (last orders)
others 10.00–18.00
Power Station Porter (4.9%)
Battersea Brewery Co., Battersea, London

In 2000 the Bankside Power Station, roughly opposite St Paul's Cathedral on the south bank of the Thames morphed into Tate Modern, Britain's national gallery of modern and contemporary art. The best way to approach it is to cross the Thames on foot via the Millennium Bridge.

Even if Picasso, Matisse, Rothko and Warhol are not your thing the huge turbine hall – art installations' answer to Wembley – might just impress as you make your way by lift to the seventh floor.

Located in a two-storey glass penthouse in black, steel and white fabric screens, added onto the original roof, there are fine views across the river and on into the crane-peppered bingo parlour known as the City of London. There are mirrored walls on the opposite side to the panoramic windows.

This being a restaurant they expect you to eat though their license allows casual drinking too. Seats are dribbled down the passageway past the café bar and along

the narrow perching bar that offers magnificent views over the Thames.

The restaurant opens for breakfast at 10.00 and remains open throughout the day, with separate lunch, afternoon tea and dinner menus that run from haddock & chips to *confit* of rabbit leg with aubergine *purée* & preserved lemon.

Hidden amid the excellence is a select list of a dozen or so bottled beers that also includes Cains Lager, Little Creatures Pale Ale, Worthington White Shield and Thomas Hardy Vintage Ale.

It is fitting that our featured beer is brewed by Battersea Brewery Company. Power Station Porter is a deep, bittersweet ruby-black beer in the tradition of this truly London beer speciality.

Victoria

10a Strathearn Place W2 2NH

T 020 7724 1191

Lancaster Gate

Sun 12.00–22.30
others 11.00–23.00

Fuller's ESB (5.5%)

Fuller Smith & Turner, Chiswick, London

The bland, pale exterior of this corner pub, housed in a four-storey building, belies the riot of colour and busy Victorian decoration inside. Feng shui it is not. This is 19th century maximalist, under the gaze of Queen Victoria and family, in a painting by court artist Franz Xaver Winterhalter.

On the ground floor is a long, narrow saloon with wooden floors, panelled walls, deep cornices and an attractive plasterwork ceiling. But the outstanding features here are the mirrors. Ornately decorated in gilt and myriad-coloured floral patterns, they make a gaudy backdrop to the bar and its imitation gas mantel lanterns.

Heavy dark green curtain drapes edged in gold brocade match dark green seating. The Prince of Wales' plume of feathers and Fleur de Lys motifs abound. Carved wooden detail is everywhere, notably in the two elegant columns and around the Georgian-style fireplace with swags, tails and urns.

Up a spiral staircase is the singular Theatre Bar, like a tiny theatre complete with false balconies, fluted columns and cloud painted ceiling. Parts were taken from the old Gaiety Theatre in the Strand.

Also upstairs is the even odder Library, a dark wood and Chesterfield-furnished bolt-hole, for all the world like a Gentlemen's Club in miniature.

Food (daily 12.00–21.30, 21.00 Sun) includes sandwiches, burgers, risotto and the ever present fish & chips, with roasts on Sunday.

The beer at the top of the Fullers' range is ESB, a brew that, like CAMRA, was born in 1971. It is a dark amber brew of great depth with a powerful toffee flavour and a warming finish.

Wenlock Arms

26 Wenlock Road N1 7TA
T 020 7608 3406
www.wenlock-arms.co.uk
➔ Old Street
🕑 Daily 12.00–24.00
🍺 **Echt Kriekenbier** (6.8%)
🍺 Brouwerij Verhaeghe, Vichte, Belgium

Nowadays this gem of a basic, traditional Victorian street corner local looks strangely out of place in a forest of modern mid-rise flats. Yet somehow it survived the best efforts of Hitler's *Luftwaffe*, well-meaning people in post-War planning and big brewery accountants to destroy this part of the capital.

Its main room is square, served by a peninsular bar, with a small parlour at the back. We are in proper pub territory here, complete with a worn floral carpet, heavy red curtains screening the lace-clad windows and blue plush banquette seating round the edges. It beats EastEnders' Old Vic, anyway.

The official Old Fogeys' club (free membership to those of pensionable age with an interest in beer) meets on Tuesday afternoons. Quiz night Thursday. Live jazz Friday and Saturday evenings plus Sunday afternoons. The pub also has both football and cricket teams.

Food (12.00–21.00) means mainly massive doorstep 'sandwedges', with salt beef the pick of the crop.

The quality of the cask ales here is so high that even in the highly competitive world of London beer pubs it has managed to keep its place in CAMRA's Good Beer Guide continuously since 1995. Nine handpulls draw an ever-changing range of traditional ales and ciders, which always includes a mild.

Ironically, our chosen beer comes in kegs from Belgium, though this minor point aside it is one of the most traditional beers in the world, being crafted by steeping whole cherries for several months in large tuns filled with oak-aged brown ale.

Echt Kriekenbier (try saying ekt-creek'n-beer) is a delicious, slightly sharp drink full of real fruit flavour but with a backdrop of great grain flavours.

White Horse

1–3 Parson's Green SW6 4UL
T 020 7736 2115
www.whitehorsesw6.com
⊖ Parson's Green
🕐 Sat 11.00–23.00; Sun 11.00–22.30
others 12.00–15.00 & 18.00–23.00
🍾 **Worthington White Shield** (5.6%)
⊞ White Shield Brewery (Coors),
Burton-upon-Trent, Staffordshire

The place that a few years back dragged London pubs into the 21st century is just a hundred yards from the tube station on Fulham's Parsons Green. Its magic mix of quality beers, good British cooking, friendly service and Victorian design make it the first stop after Heathrow for many a beer tourist.

The food (all day to 22.30) succeeds in being traditional with a modern take, innovative and high quality. Hence lentil & bacon broth, fillet of beef with champ & Savoy cabbage, fish pie and plum & cinnamon crumble. They often do barbecues on the front terrace in summer.

Eighty or so beers find their way here from around the world, in casks, kegs and bottles. The beer menu tries to keep up but enquiries will usually reveal lots of new stuff to try. They keep six cask ales, the Belgian selection includes rarities from Blaugies, Cantillon and Dupont and the US selection has highspots too.

Before its transformation, this was a Bass Charrington house famed for keeping the world-renowned Draught Bass in its cellars for several weeks before serving, to encourage natural carbonation. The company's other classic beer was Worthington White Shield, a characterful, bottle-conditioned strong pale ale.

White Shield has survived half a dozen takeovers and as many changes of brewer in the last thirty years. When Coors took over, it returned to Burton-upon-Trent, the traditional heart of UK pale ale brewing, getting its own microbrewery in the town's beer museum. As we went to press, it was being evicted once more.

Zeitgeist@The Jolly Gardeners

49–51 Black Prince Road SE11 6AB
T 020 7840 0426
www.zeitgeist-london.com
Vauxhall
Fri & Sat 12.30–01.30
others 12.00–24.00
Weihenstephan Hefeweisse Dunkel (5.3%)
Bayerische Stadtsbrauerei Weihenstephan,
Freising, Germany

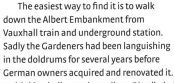

'London's first German gastro-pub' was once just the Jolly Gardeners. Charlie Chaplin's father used to play the pub piano in his Lambeth days. Guy Ritchie filmed parts of *Snatch* here back in 2000.

The easiest way to find it is to walk down the Albert Embankment from Vauxhall train and underground station. Sadly the Gardeners had been languishing in the doldrums for several years before German owners acquired and renovated it.

There are no Bavarian drinking hall paraphernalia or *Dirndl*-clad lovelies here, though you might find the *Deutches Bundesliga* showing on the two giant sports-orientated TV screens.

The Victorian design is still obvious despite the heavy black paintwork. Inside is a large island bar with a decorated back, an intensely red ceiling and a wood floor scattered with faux animal skins. You have to hoist yourself onto the giant banquettes down one side, like a Lilliputian.

Food (Mon–Sat all day to 21.30) is pan-Germanic and includes ten sorts of *schnitzel* as well as a wide selection of *wurst*, *leberkäs* with roast potatoes & fried egg, roast pork in beer sauce with dumplings & red cabbage, and herring in a cream sauce.
Does brunch (10.00–17.00) on the 1st & 3rd Sunday of the month.

Its twenty bottled beers include Früh Kölsch, Schlenkerla smoked and Schlösser Alt. Thirteen draught beers include Flensburger Pils, Köstritzer black and two from the Bavarian 'state brewery' Weihenstephan which claims to be the world's oldest.

Weihenstephan yeast adds a characteristic banana flavour to beers. The Dunkel is a hazy, deep amber wheat beer with a fruity, smooth character.